SUICIDE IN CREATIVE WOMEN

SUICIDE IN CREATIVE WOMEN

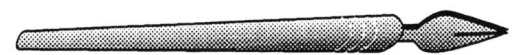

David Lester

Nova Science Publishers, Inc.

Art Director: Christopher Concannon
Graphics: Elenor Kallberg and Maria Ester Hawrys
Book Production: Michael Lyons, Roseann Pena,
　　　　　　　　Casey Pfalzer, June Martino,
　　　　　　　　Tammy Sauter, and Michelle Lalo
Circulation: Irene Kwartiroff, Annette Hellinger,
　　　　　　　and Benjamin Fung
Cover Design: Christopher Concannon

ISBN 1-56072-150-2

Lester, David, 1942-
　　Suicide in creative women / David Lester.
　　　p. cm.
　　Includes bibliographical references and index.
　　ISBN 1-56072-150-2 : $57.00
　　1. Suicide--Case studies. 2. Women Artists--Suicidal
behavior--Case studies. 3. Creative ability--Case studies.
I. Title.
HV6545.9.L47　1993　　　　　　　　　　　　93-32022
362.28'2'082--dc20　　　　　　　　　　　　　　CIP

© 1993 *Nova Science Publishers, Inc.*
　6080 Jericho Turnpike, Suite 207
　Commack, New York 11725
　Tele. 516-499-3103 Fax 516-499-3146
　E Mail Novasci1@aol.com

All rights reserved. No part of this book may be reproduced, stored in a retrieval system or transmitted in any form or by any means: electronic, electrostatic, magnetic, tape, mechanical, photocopying, recording or otherwise without permission from the publishers.

Printed in the United States of America

SUICIDE IN CREATIVE WOMEN

Table of Contents

Chapter 1 - Introduction 1

Chapter 2 - Two Painters 5
   Dora Carrington: A Suicide 5
   Kathe Kollwitz 8

Chapter 3 - Two Writers 17
   Virginia Woolf: A Suicide 17
   Dorothy Parker 22

Chapter 4 - Four Suicides 29
   Diane Arbus 29
   Sylvia Plath 35
   Anne Sexton 43
   Sara Teasdale 50

Chapter 5 - Four Nonsuicidal Creative Women 61
   Colette 61
   Amy Lowell 67
   Edna St. Vincent Millay 74
   Georgia O'Keeffe 80

Chapter 6 - Comparing the Suicidal and Nonsuicidal Women 91

Chapter 7 - Six Creative Men Who Committed Suicide 101
   John Berryman 101
   Hart Crane 111
   Mark Gertler 120
   Vachel Lindsay 127
   Cesare Pavese 136
   Mark Rothko 143

Chapter 8 - Comparing the Suicidal Women and Men 151

Index 157

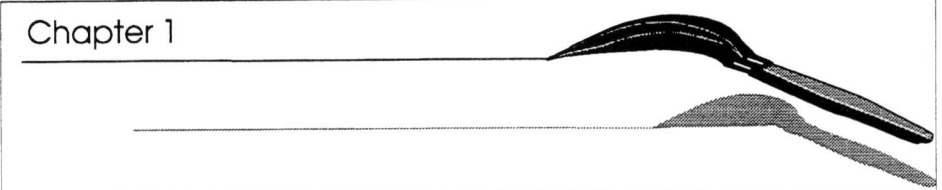

Chapter 1

INTRODUCTION

This book investigates suicide in creative women. While involved in a project exploring suicide in famous individuals for whom adequate biographies exist, I noted that suicide seemed to be especially common in writers and artists and that was true of women too. Among the suicides identified were Diane Arbus (American photographer), Dora Carrington (English painter), Anne Sexton (American poet), Sylvia Plath (American poet), Sara Teasdale (American poet), and Virginia Woolf (English writer). The question arose as to why these women committed suicide.

These were creative women. Were their suicides because they were <u>women</u>, because they were <u>creative</u>, or because they were <u>creative women</u>? It is not because they were women. As Lester (1984) has noted, in almost every nation of the world and in almost every demographic group, men engage in fatal suicidal behavior (in which the person dies) at a much higher rate than do women, while women engage in nonfatal suicidal behavior (in which the individual lives) at a much higher rate than do men. Although the total number of suicidal acts is greater in women than in men, women are <u>less</u> likely to engage in fatal suicidal acts.

Suicide in creative women may be because they are creative. Andreasen (1987) found that rates of psychiatric disorder were higher in creative writers (of both sexes) than in matched controls, especially affective disorder and perhaps the bipolar type (manic-depressive psychosis as it used to be called). A high incidence of affective disorder and creativity in the first-degree relatives of the creative writers suggested that this linkage could be genetically-mediated, but the possibility remains that creativity increases the chances of developing a psychiatric disorder. A high incidence of alcoholism has also been noted in writers (Goodwin, 1988) raising the possibility either that alcohol abuse facilitates creative writing or that creative writing increases the risk of alcohol abuse. Although formal research identified an association, the mechanisms at work remain obscure. Perhaps a detailed study of the lives of creative individuals will help us determine the causal sequence involved? The bias involved in this approach has been called *beta bias* by Hare-Mustin and Marecek (1988) since it assumes that men and women are similar.

The final possibility is that suicide in creative women is because they are both creative and women. It may be that the path of the woman who chooses to be creative is far less easy than that of a man making the same choice. The opportunities may be fewer for creative women, the prejudice against their work greater and their rewards fewer. Viewing women and men as different has been called *alpha bias* by Hare-Mustin and Marecek (1988).

In this book I will first illustrate the possibilities of looking at detailed biographies of famous creative women by comparing the lives of two painters, one of whom committed suicide (Dora Carrington) and one who did not (Käthe Kollwitz). There is, of course, some arbitrariness in picking a comparison woman since there are more creative women who have not committed suicide than women who have. Second, two writers will be compared, Virginia Woolf (who committed suicide) and Dorothy Parker (who did not but who did in her youth engage in nonfatal suicidal behavior).

Since this pairing is also arbitrary, Chapter 3 will present the lives of the remaining four suicides (Diane Arbus, Anne Sexton, Sylvia Plath and Sara Teasdale) and Chapter 4 the four nonsuicidal women (Collette [French writer], Amy Lowell [American poet], Edna St. Vincent Millay [American poet] and Georgia O'Keeffe [American painter]). In Chapter 5, the differences between these two groups of women will be discussed.

Chapter 6 will present the lives of six suicidal male creative artists, poets and writers: John Berryman (American poet), Hart Crane (American poet), Mark Gertler (English painter), Vachel Lindsay (American poet), Cesare Pavese (Italian writer) and Mark Rothko (American painter). Chapter 7 will examine the differences, if any, in the lives of the female and male suicides.

Although the choice of nonsuicidal women and suicidal men is arbitrary, some effort was made to chose both artists and writers to match the female suicides and to include non-Americans in the appropriate proportion. The test of the usefulness of my approach will, of course, be decided by the value of the conclusions which will be drawn and by the interest the process generates in you, the reader.

References

Andreasen, N. C. Creativity and mental illness. <u>American Journal of Psychiatry</u>, 1987, 144, 1288-1292.

Goodwin, D. W. <u>Alcohol and the writer</u>. Kansas City, MO: Andrews McNeel, 1988.

Hare-Mustin, R. T., & Marecek, J. Gender and the meaning of difference. <u>American Psychologist</u>, 1988, 43, 455-464.

Lester, D. Suicide. In C. S. Widom (Ed.) <u>Sex roles and psychopathology</u>. New York: Plenum, 1984, 145-156.

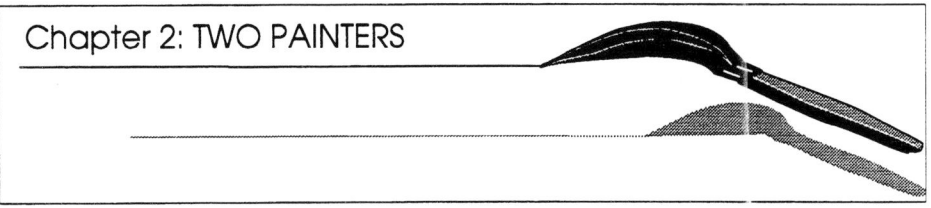

Chapter 2: TWO PAINTERS

DORA CARRINGTON: A SUICIDE [1]

Samuel Carrington was born in 1832, trained as an engineer and sailed for India in 1857. After spending thirty years there, he retired and returned to England, physically active, though slightly deaf from overdoses of quinine, taken to cure tropical diseases. In 1888, at the age of fifty-five he married Charlotte Houghton, a distant in-law. Charlotte had been a governess for her brother's children and was twenty years younger than Samuel. Her family was also of a lower social class than Samuel's. She later told people that she married Samuel out of pity and because he needed looking after.

In the next six years, Samuel and Charlotte produced five children: Lottie, Sam, Teddy, Dora and Noel. Dora was born when her father was sixty-one on March 29, 1893. Dora saw her father as a gentle man with a history of wondrous adventures, but she disliked her mother and had a poor relationship with her. Though Dora was close in age to her brother Noel, she idolized Teddy.

In her early years, the family moved frequently, but usually stayed close to London. Around the age of five, Dora suffered from incontinence. She was too shy to ask to leave the room, and she repeatedly soiled her clothes and was punished. Her feet turned inwards despite efforts to correct this. She was overweight and clumsy as a child. She was shy, rebellious, insecure and had a poor body image. When she began to menstruate she was filled with horror, and she hated the "fiend" as she called it ever after. Her mother's repressive upbringing fostered the development in Dora of a repugnance for sexual behavior.

At school Dora worked well but was not outstanding. Her spelling was poor and remained so, and she was possibly dyslexic. Because of her mother's interest in painting, Dora was introduced to art at an early age. The house always had reproductions of famous paintings on the walls,

---

1 This section is based on Gerzina (1989).

and visits to art museums were frequent. Dora showed herself to have artistic skills, and her mother was very proud of this.

When Dora was fifteen, her beloved father was paralyzed by a stroke, but apart from that her adolescence continued uneventfully. Her artistry began to find reward. She won prizes for drawing from her school and from competitions in London. Her art teacher encouraged her to apply to the Slade School of Art in London and, when she was accepted, her family was pleased to send her there. Though she remained financially dependent upon her family for many more years, her move to London began her liberation.

London Years

Dora arrived at the Slade in 1910 when she was seventeen. College life gave her freedom from her family and freedom from society's rules. Though Dora remained politically uninvolved, her life changed dramatically. At the college men and women students were on equal terms. By 1911 she was signing her name Carrington, and this is how her friends called her. She also cut off her hair, as did her friends, whereas in her home town of Bedford no woman had short hair. She often wore trousers, and she purposely developed an androgynous look. This increased the conflict between Dora and her mother when she went home for the vacations.

At the Slade, her artistic talent developed, and she was awarded a scholarship for her second year and won several of the school prizes. By 1911, she was involved in her first love triangle, with two students, Mark Gertler and Chips Nevinson. Both men sought to win Dora, and their relationships were full of conflict and tension. Gertler won, but his victory was limited. Dora had a fear or and a loathing of sexual intercourse, so that she always refused to become Gertler's lover despite his continual persistence. Mark first proposed marriage in June 1912, but he was refused.

Dora left the Slade in 1914 and at first went home. She continued to paint, and she worked for pay, painting signs, making woodcuts for the Hogarth Press (run by Leonard and Virginia Woolf) and undertaking various other artistic tasks. Through her association with the Bloomsbury circle she met Lytton Strachey, a homosexual in his midthirties and a writer who was working on his book Eminent Victorians. Lytton had a habit of falling in love with younger men who soon dropped him. One weekend, Lytton tried to kiss Dora and, in anger so the story goes, she crept into his room at night to cut off his beard. He opened his eyes and from that moment they were in love. Dora was twenty-two, Lytton thirty-five.

Life With Lytton

In 1916 Dora and Lytton went on a brief holiday together. They became lovers, though not apparently with enormous success, and they seemed to have refrained from further attempts during their life together. Dora was sharing an apartment with friends in London at the time, and she and Lytton decided to find a house together. She now became Gertler's lover, but their relationship was doomed though it limped along into 1917. She and Lytton found a house in the country and moved there in November 1917. Their life together lasted until she killed herself just one month after his death in 1932.

Their life had several threads. First, it was usually full. They continually visited and stayed with friends, both together and separately. They also had visitors to their house much of the time. They took trips abroad, together and by themselves, often with friends. They had lovers, and Dora eventually married. But she and Lytton remained intimately close all of this time. When they were apart, they wrote almost every day to each other, and their letters were full of love and affection.

Work went well. Lytton wrote and published, becoming a popular writer and earning a good income. Dora painted, and often decorated panels and objects for others. She occasionally would earn money by making paintings on glass or by painting tiles. But despite Lytton's encouragement and praise and pride in her work, she lost confidence in her artistic ability. She generally refused to exhibit her work, and she sold very few paintings during her life.

There were some losses. Although her father had a stroke in 1908, he survived until 1918. Her brother Teddy was killed during the war in 1916. But Lytton clearly took the place of her father, and his delicate health and poor digestion allowed Dora to shower attention on him as she took care of his needs.

Lytton continued his homosexual affairs, and Dora had men fall in love with her. Three of Dora's relationships are worthy of note. First, a friend of her brother's, Ralph Partidge, visited and they became attached to each other. Ralph and Lytton became friends, and soon they became a threesome. In 1921, Dora and Ralph married, and Ralph moved in with Dora and Lytton.

After several affairs, during which Ralph forbade Dora to see other men (to which edicts she surprisingly submitted), Ralph eventually fell in love with Francis Marshall, and their relationship too was incorporated into the ménage, though not without much tension. This freed Dora to have affairs too. Eventually, Ralph and Francis had their own apartment in London, but visited Dora and Lytton on weekends.

Soon Lytton rented an apartment in the same London house, and the ménage à quatre survived.

In 1923, Dora fell in love with an American woman, Henrietta Bingham, and had her first lesbian affair. Henrietta ended it late in 1924. Meanwhile, Dora was also having an affair with Gerald Brenan, a friend of her husband's.

By 1926, Dora was drinking a lot, spending weekdays alone at the country house, with her nights long and unbearable, often filled with the nightmares that had plagued her all through her life. Over the next couple of years, her fears of loneliness and aging grew stronger. Her negative feelings about her painting ability were as strong as ever. But in 1928, she met a young man, Beakus Penrose, ten years her junior, who reminded her of her brother Teddy, and they became lovers. She became pregnant by him in 1929. Ralph and Lytton knew that she would kill herself if she could not have an abortion, and so Ralph arranged one for her.

In November 1931, Lytton became seriously ill. They did not know what the problem was at the time (it was stomach cancer), and he soon died on January 22, 1932. Dora tried to kill herself using car exhaust the day before his death. Her friends knew that she planned to kill herself, and they did everything they could to prevent her from doing so. But eventually they had to leave her alone, and she shot herself wearing Lytton's robe on March 11, 1932. She survived for a few hours and told Ralph that it was an accident, which was the coroner's verdict.

Käthe Kollwitz[2]

Käthe Schmidt was born on July 8, 1867, the fifth born child of Katharina and Karl Schmidt, though two of the older children had not survived. Käthe had an older brother, Konrad, and an older sister Julie. A younger sister, Lise, came three years later, and a baby who died of meningitis a year after Lise's birth. The Schmidts lived in Konigsburg, Prussia, where her father ran a building firm.

Käthe grew into a quiet, shy and nervous child. She loved to play with other children though, being the youngest, she was often bullied. Under stress, Käthe suffered from stomach aches, was prone to violent crying and temper tantrums and, later, convulsive fits and nightmares. These outburst were typically followed by depressions which lasted for

---

[2] This section is based on Kearns (1976)

hours and sometimes days. Her mother was not physically affectionate to any of her children, and Käthe regretted this reserve. When Käthe's younger brother died, she longed to comfort her mother, but her mother's aloofness prevented her from doing so. Käthe also had fears of losing her mother, and she felt tender and solicitous toward her.

Käthe's mother was raised as a nonconformist (her father ran a group called the Free Congregation), and she was a socialist. She had artistic interests and talents and encouraged these in her children. Käthe's father was trained as a lawyer and was a member of the Social Democratic Workers Party (SPD). His political views made it difficult for him to serve the authoritarian right-wing Prussian state, and so he became a stonemason and house builder. He disapproved of the public schools and educated his children in private schools and at home. He owned a good library and encouraged the children to read. In an era when girls were not encouraged to aspire to roles other than wife/mother, Karl personally helped his daughters to develop their individual talents. Konrad seemed to like the theater, while Käthe and Lise were gifted at drawing.

Karl had dreams that Käthe would become a successful painter, and he decided to give her as much training as possible. Lise was also gifted in art, and Käthe continued to be jealous of Lise until Lise married and gave up art.

Training In Art

In 1881, at the age of fourteen, Käthe began taking art lessons with Rudolf Mauer, a local copper engraver. She learned to draw with pencil, charcoal, crayons, and pen. Also at this time, Käthe got to know some friends of her brother Konrad, Lisebeth and Karl Kollwitz, orphans who lived with a family in Konigsburg. All were members of the SPD, and the group had many political discussions. Karl Kollwitz always valued Käthe's opinions and thoughts, and Käthe enjoyed his company. At sixteen, Käthe wanted to study at Kongisburg Academy of Art but, as a female, she was not eligible. Her father paid a local painter, Emile Neide, to teach Käthe.

In the next year, 1884, Käthe's grandfather (the minister) died, and Karl Kollwitz proposed to Käthe. Käthe was not in love with Karl, but she knew he loved her. Furthermore, she knew that it would be hard to have a career as an artist if she married. Käthe's father knew this too and was opposed to the marriage. He wanted to send her away to study art.

In 1885, Käthe arrived in Berlin to study at a women's school affiliated with the Berlin Academy of Art. There, though she wanted to paint, her instructors urged her to draw. After a year, she returned to Konigsburg to study with Neide again in order to develop her skill at painting and, during the summer, her Berlin instructor died. She continued to study art and, after becoming engaged to Karl in 1889, was sent to Munich to study by her father who still hoped to keep his daughter from marrying. The Munich Academy had a women's school attached to it, and Käthe studied painting there. The fellow women students considered marriage an act of betrayal, for in their eyes one could not be a wife and an artist. When they learned of Käthe's engagement, they attacked her for it, but she held her silence and kept to her decision. The students formed a composition club so they could paint with more freedom than permitted in the classes. They met regularly at a small cafe which hung their work on its walls. Käthe also joined a etching club where she began to learn the technical skills that served her well in her artistic career. Käthe loved the lengthy careful process required for etching which fitted her creative style better than painting. Käthe stayed a second year in Munich to study, but returned to Konigsburg a little disappointed in her progress, especially in painting.

Karl Kollwitz had finished medical school and interned in Berlin. He was chosen to implement a plan of social and medical insurance for workers there, and this appealed to his and Käthe's political views. Käthe then had to choose between staying at home, supported by her father, and marrying Karl and trying to build a career despite being a wife. (Working as an newspaper illustrator, the only job for which she was skilled, was not open to women.) She saw that her father would stifle her creativity, urging her to paint genre paintings for exhibits. So she chose marriage and sought to show her father that she could be a wife and an artist.

Karl found an apartment in a tenement in a working class neighborhood section of Berlin, a tenement in which they lived for fifty years, and they married on June 13, 1891. Karl worked hard at the clinic, and Käthe worked hard drawing. She spent much time talking to, counseling and drawing the working class women who came to the clinic, and the Kollwitz's were soon accepted into the community.

Käthe's first major project was a series of lithographs and etchings celebrating the revolt of a group of Silesian weavers in 1844. The series took her five years, and it established her as a socialist artist whose works would celebrate and support the workers in their political struggles. Her efforts to show her work met with failure at first, but the rejected artists decided to hold their own show. Käthe's works were criticized by one commentator (simply because Käthe was female) and praised by another. The artists struggling for recognition formed a group called <u>Die Sezession</u> (The Secession), with Käthe the only female member, which organized its own shows and exhibits.

Käthe became pregnant that first autumn, and Hans was born in May 1892. The Kollwitzs hired a live-in housekeeper, Lina Makler, about Käthe's age, who stayed with them and helped them to run the house and home for the rest of her life. A second son, Peter, was born in 1896. Käthe's father became that ill that year and died in the following year, but he was overjoyed to see his daughter's work, especially the series on the Weavers' revolt. The series was shown in Great Berlin Exhibit in 1898 and created a sensation. Kaiser Wilhelm II vetoed giving a woman the gold medal, but the next year the King of Saxony awarded Käthe the gold medal for her works at the Dresden exhibit. At the age of thirty two, Käthe was counted among the foremost artists of Germany.

The Mature Artist

Although Käthe never worked for the left-wing political parties of her era, she drew for them. A series of etchings which she completed in 1900 dramatized the waste of workers' lives as a result of the social conditions. Another series commemorated the Peasant War of 1525. Many of her drawings were used for posters, though often the government ordered the posters removed.

She was asked to teach at the Berlin School of Art for Women, but the work interfered with her household chores and her drawing, and so she stopped teaching. Her children were ill frequently, Hans with diphtheria and Peter with many lung infections. But in her 30s, Hans's brush with death was the only personal trauma.

In 1904, she visited Paris by herself and came back with and raised the eleven year-old son, Georg Gretor, of a Munich classmate living there in poverty. In 1907, a former teacher awarded her a prize to study in Florence, and she enjoyed her stay there despite her dislike of Italian art. She and a women friend (who carried a gun in case of danger) hiked one hundred and fifty miles to Rome, after which their husbands and children joined them for the summer.

Käthe completed the etchings for the Peasant War in 1908. The final frame, *Prisoners*, was used for a revolutionary poster in Ireland in 1972 (with the legend "No More Internment"), attesting to its lasting appeal. This series confirmed Käthe's stature as one of the great graphic artists. Käthe also worked as a free-lance artist for the magazine <u>Simplizissimus</u>.

Like her mother, Käthe rarely showed physical affection to her family, and she kept her thoughts and feelings to herself. Perhaps to compensate for this, she began keeping a journal in 1908. In it she often worried about her periods of depression, though they were typically followed by (shorter) periods of productivity.

Käthe's son Peter fell ill in the winter of 1910-1911, and his parents sent him to a sanatorium. He then went to work as a farmhand in Poland. He also began to show an interest in painting. Hans went off to the University of Freiberg. Käthe, meanwhile, was troubled by irregular menstruation and then by menopause. She felt insecure about her work, and she sometimes destroyed works which had taken her weeks to create. She was often overwhelmed by apathy and depression and a sense of futility.

When the First World War broke out, Peter volunteered to fight and was quickly killed in the fighting in Belgium. Käthe was overcome by her grief, but she eventually came out of it by resolving to create a monument to honor Peter and the other young men who had fallen in the war. She had tried her hand at sculpting many years earlier, and she decided to sculpt the monument.

Honors continued to be awarded to Käthe. In 1916 she was chosen as a juror for the New Secession art group, and in 1917 her fiftieth birthday was celebrated with a retrospective show, a show which was highly praised. In 1919, Käthe became the first woman elected to a full professorship at the Prussian Academy of Arts, a position which provided her with a large fully-equipped studio. (She was promoted to head of a department there in 1928, thereby becoming a full-time Prussian civil servant.) She continued to work on the five themes which interested her: herself, mothers and children, the life of the proletariat, death as a force, and war. Käthe's own mother was now senile and lived with the Kollwitz's. Käthe enjoyed having her mother with her and taking care of her as she grew weaker. Käthe's mother died in February, 1925.

Käthe's work continued to be popular, and she was commissioned to do memorial and posters for socialist causes. In 1926, Käthe helped found GEDOK, a society which sponsored women artists. She received so much mail from admirers that she had to hire a secretary to help her answer the letters. The 1920s proved to be one of the most productive periods of her life. The International Trade Union Congress in Amsterdam commissioned a poster in 1923 and the organizers of the Central German Youth Day in Leipzig in 1924. Her work was exhibited in Moscow, and the Soviet Union invited her to visit in 1927.

In 1926 the Kollwitz's visited the Belgium cemetery where Peter was buried, and by 1931 she had completed the monuments. After exhibiting them in Berlin, they were shipped and placed in the cemetery in Belgium.

In 1933, Käthe's world began to disintegrate. Hitler was in power. The Nazis forced Käthe and other socialist colleagues to resign from the Berlin Academy, and the Nazis soon banned all exhibits of her work.

In July 1933, Käthe was interrogated by the Gestapo because of an interview she had given in a magazine but, though Käthe and her husband Karl lived in fear of further interrogation and imprisonment, the Gestapo left them alone thereafter. The Nazis forbade Karl to practice medicine and, from that time on, Käthe and Karl carried vials of poison with them in case they were taken into custody.

On her seventieth birthday, Käthe received more than 150 letters and telegrams from all over the world. An American collector purchased some of her work, providing helpful commissions. He also offered her asylum in America, but Käthe decided to stay in Germany with her family. Karl became quite ill and died in July 1940.

Käthe lived with her old housekeeper, Lina, and her niece who helped to take care of her. In October 1942, her grandson was killed in the fighting. The bombing of Berlin was so severe in 1943 that a young sculptor persuaded Käthe to move into the country with her at Nordhausen. Six months after she moved there, her old house in Berlin was destroyed by bombs. Prince Ernst Heinrich of Saxony offered her refuge at his estate in Moritzburg near Dresden. There she suffered heart failure, and she died April 22, 1945, four months before the end of the war.

Discussion

Neither of these women appeared to have psychiatric disturbances. Neither were psychotic at any period in their lives, showed neurotic symptoms or could be said to have had a personality disorder, and neither abused alcohol or other drugs.

Dora was not seriously depressed in her life, and she seemed to have weathered her interpersonal crises quite well. In her late thirties, though, old age and the prospect of a loveless life filled her with dread. Although her social life could have been full, she preferred to spend weekdays alone and lonely in the country. However, she and Lytton felt especially close during his last year, and their feelings for each other were stronger than ever. A few days before his death he called for her and said:

> Darling Carrington. I love her. I always wanted to
> marry Carrington and never did. (Gerzina, 1989, p. 293)

Käthe was depressed from time to time during her life, but she knew that her depressions would lift and be replaced by periods of creative productivity. Certainly, her depressions seemed not to have interfered much at all with her day-to-day functioning.

Interestingly, both Dora and Käthe had parents, and more surprisingly, fathers who were proud of and who encouraged their daughters' artistic talents. Käthe, living in earlier times (and perhaps because she lived in Germany) encountered more resistance to women as artists, but she seems to have faced this prejudice and not allowed it to affect her work or her aspirations.

Both Dora and Käthe had problems with sexuality. Dora had both male and female lovers. Käthe is described by her biographer as having bisexual feelings though probably not ever taking a lover other than her husband. The striking difference, of course, is that Käthe married, raised children, and developed a good supportive relationship with her husband, while Dora seems to have escaped heterosexual commitment by living with Lytton Strachey. Her marriage was not out of mature heterosexual love, and she could not face having a child.

Though Käthe often felt inadequate as an artist and doubted her talent, she continued to work, and her work was always praised. Dora, on the other hand, lost confidence in her artistic talent once she began to live with Lytton, and she gave up pursuit of a career in art. With no career, survival without Lytton was perhaps too meaningless and too unpleasant to contemplate.

Dora had never threatened suicide before (except when pregnant), nor attempted it. Yet her friends knew that she would kill herself after Lytton's death. Lytton appears to have been the single part of her existence that made life worthwhile. Without him, there was nothing for her. Käthe survived the death of her son in the First World War, aided perhaps by the presence of her husband and older son, and later the death of her husband. Of course, Karl died in 1940, when Käthe was seventy three and near the end of her natural life.

Thus, the most noteworthy difference between these two painters is the over-dependency that Dora developed with Lytton in contrast to the less pathological relationship that Käthe had with Karl. What is puzzling is that, although Dora's childhood was perhaps a little more traumatic than Käthe's, with more severe problems in self-esteem and self-confidence, modern suicidologists would not predict a suicidal outcome for Dora.

References

Gerzina, A. <u>Carrington</u>. New York: Norton, 1989.
Kearns, M. <u>Käthe Kollwitz</u>. Old Westbury, NY: Feminist Press, 1976.

Chapter 3: TWO WRITERS

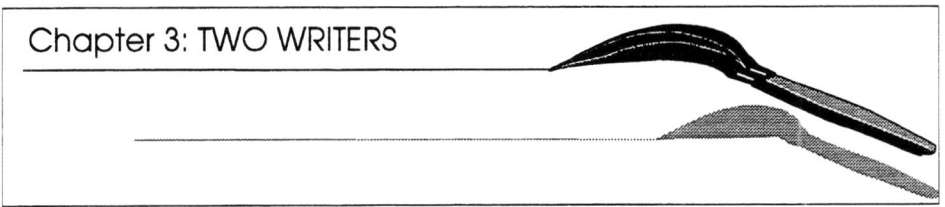

Virginia Woolf: A Suicide

Virginia Woolf was a leading literary figure in Great Britain in the early part of this Century. She wrote novels, book reviews for newspapers and magazines and literary criticism. She drowned herself in the River Ouse on March 28th, 1941 at the age of 59. The present section is based on a biography written by her nephew, Quentin Bell (1972).

Her Parents And Early Years

The Stephens were originally a family of farmers and merchants from Aberdeenshire in Scotland. Her grandfather was first a lawyer, but then joined the Civil Service in the Colonial Office, working hard for the abolition of slavery. He wrote for the Edinburgh Review and other journals. He was shy, pessimistic, convinced of his ugliness, and prone to deny himself any pleasure. If he found something he liked (like cigars or snuff), he avoided it altogether.

His youngest surviving child was a son, Leslie. Leslie was a nervous delicate boy, his mother's darling, and fond of poetry. He went to Cambridge University and later accepted a fellowship there, becoming an ordained minister in the process which was a pre-requisite for the position. However, he was dissatisfied by life there and moved to London where he worked as a journalist. He eventually became editor of the Dictionary of National Biography.

His first wife was Harriet Thackeray, daughter of the novelist. They had a daughter Laura, who was soon noticed to be psychologically disturbed.[1] Harriet died in childbirth in 1875, on Leslie's forty-third birthday. Leslie soon became close to a friend of his wife, Julia Jackson (Duckworth), recently widowed and with three children. They married on

---

[1] She died in an asylum in 1945.

March 26, 1878. They already had four children by their first spouses, and they had two more, a daughter Vanessa and a son Thoby. They planned to have no more children, but two more were born, Virginia and Adrian.

Virginia was born January 25, 1882 in London, into the upper middle classes, though Bell places the family at the lower division of this particular class. (They had seven maidservants but no manservants. They sometimes traveled in a cab but did not keep a carriage.)

Virginia was a pretty child and, though she was slow in leaning to talk, soon showed a precocious brilliance. The children decided that Vanessa would be a painter and Virginia a writer. Virginia was later described as eccentric, prone to accidents, witty and easily provoked to furious rages by her brothers and sisters. Virginia, who had become the story teller in the nursery, started a family newspaper in 1891 which she produced weekly for four years.

Childhood was relatively uneventful. They all got whooping cough in 1888 from which they recovered, though Virginia seemed weaker afterwards. The boys were sent off to school, while the girls were educated at home by their parents and then by a succession of governesses and tutors. They learnt drawing, dancing, music, and languages. They vacationed in St Ives, Cornwall.

Since we know that Virginia eventually became psychiatrically disturbed, it is important to look for portents of madness in the family. In 1891, Laura was still living at home. A cousin, J. K. Stephen, received brain damage in an accident in 1886 and subsequently showed signs of madness, in particular manic euphoria and excitement. Virginia's father had very poor health. He collapsed in 1888, 1890, and 1891. He suffered from insomnia, what he called "fits of the horrors", and worries about his finances.

In 1895, Virginia's mother caught influenza. It was followed by rheumatic fever, and she died on May 5th, 1895. Virginia was thirteen. Her father was sixty-three, a widower for the second time. His grief was great, and he broke down frequently in front of his children. His stepdaughter, Stella, stepped in to take over the family and comfort Leslie. The oldest of the step-children, George, now twenty-seven, began at this time to molest Virginia (and continued to do so until she was twenty-two).

Adolescence and the First Breakdown

Virginia's first 'breakdown' occurred in the summer of 1895 soon after her mother's death. Later she remembered the excitability and nervousness, the intolerable depression, a fear of meeting people and hearing voices. She stopped writing the family newspaper.

Stella became engaged in 1896 and was married in April, 1897. She became ill with peritonitis and died in July. Virginia's health deteriorated during this period. There was a fear of going out in the street, as well as a fever and rheumatic pains, but not a complete breakdown. Soon she was back at lessons, learning Greek and Latin.

Leslie's hearing was deteriorating, and a lot of his friends had died. However, he recovered from his grief, though he remained chronically melancholy. He encouraged the literary interests of his family and turned to Vanessa to run the family. He continued to worry about finances which made life hard for Vanessa who had to fight with him for money to run the household.

Thoby went to Cambridge, and Vanessa and Virginia were introduced to his friends, many of whom later became the nucleus of an intellectual group centered around the Stephens' children and known as the Bloomsbury group. Vanessa made more of an effort to 'come out' in society than Virginia, but both thoroughly disliked this and withdrew from the activities as soon as they could.

On Their Own As Adults

Leslie died after a long illness in February 1904. In May, Virginia had her second breakdown. She heard voices, distrusted Vanessa and her nurses, tried to starve herself and grieved for her father. She tried to kill herself by jumping from a window which was not high enough for her to do much harm. As she recovered, the mental symptoms lessened, leaving her with headaches and neuralgia.

The three children decided to move into a house in Bloomsbury by themselves. They began to have 'At Homes' on Thursday evenings to which many intellectual friends came. Virginia published her first piece in The Guardian at the end of 1904, and in 1905 she began her association with The Times Literary Supplement. She taught briefly at an evening institute for working men. Then in 1906 on a trip to Greece, Vanessa and Thoby both became ill. Vanessa recovered, but Thoby was misdiagnosed as having malaria and died in November with typhoid fever. Vanessa became engaged to Clive Bell two days later. Interestingly during these crises, Virginia functioned well and without any breakdown, though she missed Thoby greatly.

After Vanessa's marriage, Virginia and Adrian moved into a smaller house, and their life continued much as before with Thoby's friends as theirs and with activities being split between their household and the Bell's. Virginia's writing was successful, and she began working on a novel in addition to writing for literary magazines. Virginia also began seriously to think of marriage for the first time.

Hitherto, Virginia had been attached mainly to women, especially Violet Dickinson, who seemed to have been in love with Virginia and vice versa, though the relationship was not sexual. Virginia's first flirtation was with an older family friend, Walter

Headlam, but the interest soon petered out, and he died unexpectedly in June 1908, causing her some grief.

Virginia was physically ill and close to another breakdown in 1910 but recovered after a rest cure. She turned down a proposal of marriage from Lytton Strachey (who was homosexual) and resisted the attention of her brother-in-law, Clive. [2] After rejecting several suitors, in 1911, an old friend, Leonard Woolf, returned on leave from Ceylon and fell in love with Virginia. After another bout with exhaustion in 1912, Virginia agreed to marry Leonard. The wedding took place in August, 1912.

Mrs. Woolf

Virginia's life with Leonard was full, but also relatively uneventful. They lived happily together, started a publishing company (the Hogarth Press), and worked hard. Virginia wrote and wrote, eventually amassing a considerable body of work, including novels that were received with critical acclaim.

Their life quickly developed into a routine. Leonard took care of Virginia, especially during her breakdowns, but also between breakdowns as he tried to prevent their reoccurrence. They wrote most mornings, walked in the afternoons, and read in the evenings. They entertained and were entertained in return.

Virginia was frigid which was ascribed to her experiences with her half-brother. Virginia wanted to have children, though Leonard did not. After much consultation with specialists, the majority opinion was that it was too dangerous for her to have any.

Her first novel (The Voyage Out) was accepted in 1913, though it was not published until March 1915. However, its acceptance led to another breakdown. She had anxieties about her writing talent, sleepless nights, headaches, depression, a sense of guilt, an aversion to food, and fears that people were laughing at her. In September, 1913, Virginia took a lethal dose of veronal, but after having her stomach pumped, she survived - barely. As she recovered, her manias returned, and she went from depression to violent excitement. [3] Leonard considered putting her into an asylum, but rejected the idea, and slowly she began to recover, though with a relapse in February 1915 just before her novel appeared.

The reviews of her novel were positive, and her recovery progressed. Virginia's novels were very close to her own private world,

---

[2.] Many of the men in the Bloomsbury circle were gay, and Virginia's attraction to them may have been increased by her fear of (and inexperience with) sex, sensitized as she had been by her earlier experiences of sexual molestation.

[3.] Leonard, and others, later diagnosed Virginia's disorder as a manic-depressive psychosis.

and she was aware that they might be seen as crazy (or really be crazy). If they had been mocked, then this would have been a mockery of her true self. Praise for her novels was a certificate of sanity.

Her Death

Virginia had breakdowns in June 1921 (after a mild depression in August 1919 just before the publication of Night And Day), and mild ones in August 1926, September 1929, May 1936. She had frequent periods of total exhaustion, notably January 1922, September 1925, and July 1933, as well as many less severe illnesses.[4]

All of her novels caused her anxiety and depression, especially during the time between the completion of writing and the appearance of the book. Also, beginning in 1934, her style was seen by critics as old-fashioned, and criticism became more common.

As she grew older, more and more friends died. Kitty Maxse killed herself in 1922 and Dora Carrington in 1932. Lytton Strachey died in 1932 and her nephew Julian in 1937 in the Spanish Civil War.

The Second World War also created intense stress for Virginia. (Leonard was Jewish.) They discussed suicide in May 1940, and decided to keep enough gasoline on hand (and later morphia) to kill themselves.

She finished a final novel (Between The Acts) in November 1940. By January 1941, Leonard was very alarmed by her psychological state. On the morning of Friday March 28, 1941, Virginia wrote suicide notes and walked to the River Ouse where she put a large stone into her coat pocket and drowned herself (possibly already having tried to drown herself at an earlier time). In her letter to Leonard, she explained:

> I feel certain I am going mad again. I feel we can't go through another of those terrible times. And I shan't recover this time. (Bell, 1972, p. 226)

[4.] September 1922, January 1923, January 1925, January 1926, June 1927, January 1928, January 1929, February 1930, August 1930, May 1931, November 1931, July 1932, November 1932, February 1934, May 1934, October 1934, January 1936, November 1937, January 1938, April 1939, and February 1940. Many of these illnesses were accompanied by or the result of Winter influenzas.

Dorothy Parker

Dorothy's Early Years[5]

Dorothy was born on August 22 1893 to Mrs. Henry Rothschild. Unfortunately, Mrs. Rothschild was on holiday at the New Jersey shore at the time, and Dorothy was two months premature.

The Rothschilds were not related to the Rothschilds, although Mr. Rothschild had been successful in the garment industry and lived in a good neighborhood in the West Seventies in Manhattan, waited on by servants. Mr. Rothschild was Jewish, but his wife was Scottish.

Dorothy found no love in her home. She had an older sister and an older brother but seems not to have been close to them. Her mother died during her infancy. Her father remarried, but Dorothy never felt close to or liked her stepmother. She also seems to have been terrified of her father.

Her stepmother was Catholic and took pains to have Dorothy brought up as a Catholic. She sent her to nearby Catholic school run by nuns where Dorothy felt like an outsider. Dorothy hated being a Jew. She hated her name, and she grew to hate herself.

Dorothy developed two sides to her personality. Outwardly, she became well-mannered and pretty (with beautiful dark hair and large eyes that always seemed close to tears), a feminine dissembler. Inside was an angry, truth-seeking rebellious mind, appraising the world with ruthless accuracy.

For high school, she was fortunate in being sent to Miss Dana's School in Morristown, New Jersey. It was one of the best boarding schools in the nation. Leading women's colleges waived the examination requirement for students from the school. Although after graduation in 1911 Dorothy did not go to college, she acquired a sound education while at the school, not only in classical studies but in current affairs.

The Young Adult

Dorothy's first few years after high school are not well documented. Her father died when she was nineteen. Soon after leaving high school, she found herself a room in a boarding house in Manhattan. She spent some time writing and supported herself by playing the piano for a dancing school.

[5.] This section is based on Keats (1970).

She had a poem accepted by <u>Vogue</u> in 1916, and the editor gave her a job. Now her days were full. She had two jobs and continued to write and submit her poems. In 1917 she was promoted to <u>Vanity Fair</u>, and she also married Edwin Parker.

Edwin Parker worked as a broker in Wall Street. He was an Anglo-Saxon Protestant from an old, religious Hartford family, and they fell in love. However, on March 4, 1917, America declared war on Germany, and Eddie enlisted, ending up in the ambulance corps.

While he was in America, Dorothy visited him on weekends at the camps where he was, or Eddie would come to Manhattan. But then, eventually he was sent to Europe. Their marriage had consisted of nine months of weekends and then letter-writing. Dorothy wrote to him every day. After the war, Eddie was assigned to occupation duty in the Rhineland.

Meanwhile, Robert Benchley and Robert Sherwood joined <u>Vanity Fair</u>, and Dorothy would go with them for lunch to the Algonquin Hotel, starting a lunch group of talented young men and women that over the years became famous (later including Franklin Pierce Adams, Alexander Woollcott and Harold Ross).

This group assisted in the metamorphosis of Dorothy. In 1919, there was no radio or television, and so newspapers were widely read and very influential. Adams's column was one of the most popular newspaper columns, and he began to report on Dorothy's witticisms at lunch (and her evening outings) to his readers. Soon Dorothy Parker had a reputation as the wittiest woman in New York. This reputation, combined with a life-style in which she smoked, worked for a living, took lunch and went unchaperoned to the theater with other women's husbands, also set her apart as one of the New Women.

The Algonquin group did not discuss each other's work. Their conversation was witty and superficial. They went to parties, the theater and speakeasies. Unlike those leading a Bohemian life, the group was not revolting against society - they felt superior to it. Of course, the wittiness was often hostile, especially toward those who were not with the group at the time. The humor turned to banter, and the banter to insult.

Eddie returned in August 1919, after a separation of fifteen months. He did not fit in well with the Algonquin crowd, and he soon began to drop out of the social life of the group. By 1920, Eddie was drinking heavily. He wanted to move back to Hartford, but Dorothy refused. She loved life in New York and felt that her in-laws disliked her for having a Jewish father. She soon moved out to her own apartment. (Eddie permitted Dorothy to divorce him in 1926 for cruelty and to retain his name.)

Dorothy was fired early in 1920 from <u>Vanity Fair</u>, and the two Roberts (Benchley and Sherwood) resigned in protest. They soon got other jobs, but Dorothy remained unemployed. She also seemed to have stopped writing. (It always seemed to others that writing was a distasteful chore for Dorothy.) Little happened in 1920 or 1921. But in 1922 she fell in love again.

Unfortunately, she fell in love with Charles MacArthur, a young newspaperman and a womanizer. But now her writing could proceed again. Her pieces appeared in the leading magazines, and she and friends wrote a revue (No, Siree!) that ran for a month.

As her relationship with Charles began to ebb, she discovered she was pregnant. She had an abortion, and soon afterwards attempted suicide. She was home in her apartment and asked for food to be sent up. When the waiter arrived, he found her in the bathroom with her wrists slashed. Some of her friends thought she intended this as a gesture; others thought it was a sign of her disorganization and impulsiveness. After this, she began to drink more.

At thirty, Dorothy was still beautiful. She was also neither married, divorced, nor celibate. She lived in a cheap apartment building, with no close female friends. (Later in life, she would be close to Beatrice Ames and a few other women.) She was witty and a good writer, but in 1924 she hardly wrote.

By 1925 she was writing the poems that would be in her first book Enough Rope, some sweet and poignant, others flippant and ironic, ranging from black to blue. But she also attempted suicide again, this time more seriously. Robert Benchley and others found her in her apartment, comatose from an overdose of drugs. One of her stanzas from this period is:

> If wild my breast and sore my pride,
> I bask in dreams of suicide;
> If cool my heart and high my head,
> I think, "How lucky are the dead!"

Her next lover was Seward Collins, heir to a national chain of tobacco shops, a patron of the arts who adored her. In 1926 they went to France to meet the American intellectuals living in Paris, ending up with the Murphy's on the French Riviera. Dorothy and Seward quarreled during the trip, and Seward left for America. Dorothy stayed on till October, arriving home with a best selling book - of poems no less. Soon she was an enormous success, contributing to The New Yorker and The Bookman, well-publicized and talked-about.

Dorothy began to tire a little of her group. It seemed trivial; it lacked any meaning. She began to get involved with political issues, supporting Sacco and Vanzetti, anarchists accused of murder committed during a payroll robbery. They were executed on her thirty-fourth birthday. In 1928, her second book of poems was published, and she was involved with a businessman, John Garrett. But she was beginning to write the short stories on which her claim to literary stature would be based. "Big Blonde" won the national O. Henry Prize as the best short story in 1929.

She next had an affair with John McClain, a clerk on Wall Street, had an appendectomy which, despite her income, she couldn't pay for. (Dorothy always had to rely on her friends to manage her life.) She pursued gaiety and drank heavily. (She even went to Alcoholics

Anonymous for one meeting, and her biographer, Keats, considers Dorothy to have been an alcoholic.)

Life With Alan

In 1932, Dorothy met Alan Campbell. In 1933 she married him. He was twenty-nine, and she was forty. Alan was also half Jewish and half Scottish. Alan was a minor actor, aware that his talents were meager. He had hopes of taking Dorothy to Hollywood where they could work together on movie scripts.

Life with Alan soon fell into a pattern. They had fun but quarreled a lot. They even got divorced for one period but remarried. They worked well together on scripts. Between 1933 and 1938, they received screen credits for fifteen films, including "A Star Is Born" and earned lots of money that they quickly spent. They drank heavily, and Dorothy put on weight.

Alan liked Hollywood, but Dorothy did not. This led to frequent sojourns to New York, followed by trips back to Hollywood. For a while they owned a house in Bucks County, near Philadelphia (where she miscarried after three months of pregnancy), and commuted across country to Hollywood.

Although Dorothy said that she was happy during this time, Keats describes her as ".....living with a fretful husband in a rather oddly furnished house, quarreling with her friends, allowing herself to grow dumpy in barren middle age, wasting her time on silly scripts, stunning herself with alcohol and sleeping pills....."

Dorothy took up the anti-Nazi cause in the Spanish Civil War, even calling herself a communist. She went to Spain in 1937 to view the war from the Loyalist side. (The result, of course, was the blacklisting of both her and Alan in the 1940s and 1950s during America's hysterical anti-communist witch-hunt.)

Alan joined the Air Force, and Dorothy was both proud of him and scared of him going off to war as Eddie had in the First World War. She followed Alan from camp to camp in America, as she had with Eddie, until he was sent to Europe. After victory, Alan stayed in London. Dorothy told friends he was involved in a homosexual affair. (She had accused him of homosexual leanings throughout their marriage.) And she divorced him. But this time, there were no suicide attempts.

Dorothy published nothing in 1945 and 1946. But after the divorce in 1947, she collaborated on a story, a play and a film script with her lover (Ross Evans). In 1949, after being dumped by Ross, she called Alan who had returned to Hollywood, and they decided to get back together.

After they remarried in 1950, they lived in Hollywood, but they separated after two years, and Dorothy went back to New York, where she lived at the Volney Hotel with other lonely aging ladies. But three years later, Alan visited her in New York and persuaded her to return to Hollywood to work on a movie script with him. The movie was never produced, and that was the last script they ever worked on. They lived on their unemployment checks (of $300 a month each) until Dorothy was hired by Esquire to write book reviews for $750 a month. (Esquire continued to pay her this each month until she died, regardless of whether she sent them any reviews.) [6]

After seven years in their small house in a seedy section of Los Angeles, Dorothy woke up one morning (June 13, 1963) to find Alan dead beside her. Dorothy was sixty-nine. She returned to New York, to the Volney Hotel where she stayed until she died.

Her last article appeared in the November 1964 issue of Esquire. She visited her old friend, Beatrice Ames, for dinners. Friends visited her but were often appalled by her drunken state and the squalor of the rooms. She eventually began to lose her sight. She died at the age of seventy-three on June 7, 1967, of a heart attack.

Her death merited an obituary on Page 1 and almost all of Page 38 of The New York Times.

Discussion

Virginia Woolf clearly had recurrent mental breakdowns during her life. It is likely that she indeed suffered from a manic-depressive psychosis, with periods of both depression and mania. She also heard voices and had some phobic behaviors concerned with eating (even when she was not psychotic). Her breakdowns seemed to have occurred after two types of events: severe loss (for example, after the death of her mother) and after completing a novel and waiting for its publication.

She experienced the death of her mother when she was thirteen, an age at which loss seems to be especially critical for later suicides (Lester, 1989). In addition, recent research has documented the increased risk of suicide in those physically and sexually abused as children (Lester, 1992).

She was also prone to exhaustion, and her family thought that this was brought on by too much social activity. Typically, a rest cure was prescribed. This exhaustion seemed to facilitate the appearance of a breakdown.

Her suicide note asserted that she was killing herself because she was scared of suffering another breakdown, one with no recovery, and because of the effect of her illnesses on Leonard. Some people go mad to prevent themselves committing suicide; others commit suicide because of their fear of mental illness. Virginia seems to be among the latter.

The question that remains is one of timing. Why in 1941? She almost died in her suicide attempt soon after her marriage when her

---

6. She did review 208 books for them, however.

literary career was still in its infancy. By 1941, however, her novels were receiving increasing criticism, and she feared that she would not be able to write again. The war, with its threats for Leonard, was also a new stress. (Their house in London was damaged by bombs.) She was fifty-nine, perhaps no longer possessing the resiliency of her youth.

She was an agnostic, without religious beliefs that might inhibit her taking her own life. This time, too, there was no attending physician to advise them. Leonard persuaded a friend who was physician to see Virginia. But apart from this one consultation, there was no doctor, therapist or nurse on hand. Four days before her suicide, Virginia wrote to her publishers asking that her novel not be published, indicating that her typical fears about publishing were still strong.

If she had been able to survive this latest breakdown, would she have recovered as she had in the past, and would she eventually have killed herself, perhaps during the next crisis? She was a chronically depressed person, with a history of suicidal preoccupation, and she might have killed herself at any time. It is perhaps a surprise that she lived so long.

Dorothy Parker's early adult life in Manhattan and her public reputation as a witty liberated woman obscured the other side of Dorothy. Her written work expressed her sadness and bitterness, especially about the lot of women. Despair lay behind most of her actions and writing. Her biographer describes her poems as ".....portraying a woman who said she was suspicious of joy, disillusioned as to love, contemptuous of and sorry for herself, and given to thoughts of death."

Later, after twenty-nine so-so years with Alan, Keats describes her as ".....crouched in silence, writing virtually nothing and drinking more than she ate, talking more to her poodle than with those who would be her friends, discontent with her present and dissatisfied with her memories of the past....."

Not a happy soul. Yet, she had a gritty determination to go on and could never quench her hope.

Her childhood was miserable - a mother dead early and a home with no love, only a harsh father and an eccentric step-mother, and schools where she felt an outsider. (She made no friends from those years, and her family had no place in her later life.)

Her two suicide attempts (some friends reported at least five) were in her late twenties and early thirties. Charles MacArthur had abandoned her, leaving her to have an abortion prior to her first suicidal gesture. Her second attempt two years later was more serious, but Keats gives no immediate precipitating cause.

What is more curious is that in later life, romantic loss and living alone did not lead to suicide attempts. Her classic poem on methods of suicide had concluded that "....you might as well live." And so she did. But why?

The differences between Dorothy Parker and Virginia Woolf are immediately clear. Virginia seems to have had a slightly more stable home life, though she did lose her mother when she was thirteen and was sexually abused. She married late in life, but had a stable and happy marriage (asexual though it might have been).

Virginia was much more of an intellectual than Dorothy. She wrote serious reviews of literature. She wrote novels that received critical acclaim rather than popular success. The Bloomsbury group discussed intellectual matters and was not simply a social group for witty repartee. Dorothy's was the life of those who ape the intellectuals. The theater, but not the symphony or the opera. Drinking at speakeasies rather than gathering at friends' houses for talk.

With her husband, Virginia founded the Hogarth Press which published works such as those by Sigmund Freud. Dorothy and her husband wrote Hollywood scripts. But Dorothy was isolated from her family, without female friends, and alone in New York. The Algonquin group was her only group.

Yet the most important difference between Virginia and Dorothy was that Virginia clearly had a bipolar affective disorder from an early age whereas Dorothy seemed to be free from psychiatric disorder. The more disturbed of the two made the more serious suicidal act.

Virginia killed herself because of her fear of mental illness, while Dorothy lived on to an old age, not particularly happy but not too unhappy. At least the alcohol could blunt the pain of living, and for most of her middle and old age there was Alan to quarrel with and structure her life around. One might as well live.

References

Bell, Q. Virginia Woolf. New York: Harcourt Brace Jovanovich, 1972.
Keats, J. You might as well live. New York: Simon & Schuster, 1970.
Lester, D. Experience of personal loss and later suicide. Acta Psychiatrica Scandinavica, 1989, 79, 450-452.
Lester, D. Why people kill themselves. Springfield, IL: Charles Thomas, 1992.

Chapter 4

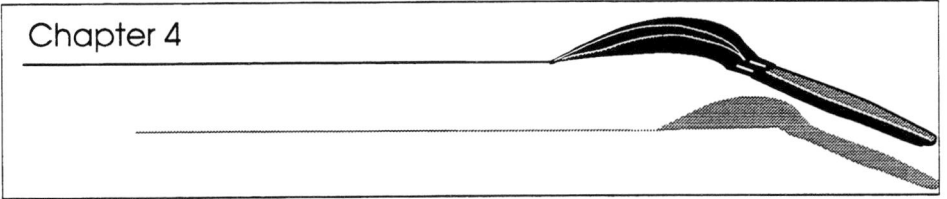

FOUR SUICIDES

In previous chapters we have compared the lives of two female painters and two female writers, one of each pair making a fatal suicidal act and one not. In this chapter we will present the lives of the remaining four creative women who committed suicide.

Diane Arbus[1]

Diane's Jewish maternal grandfather emigrated to the USA from Poland and eventually became a bookie in New York City. He got into the fur trade as something to do in the winter when the racetracks were closed. He opened a fur store on 14th Street in Manhattan. One of his daughters, Gertrude, fell in love with a boy, David Nemerov, who had started at the store as a window dresser and, against her parents' wishes, married him. In time David rose to become the head of the company.

Three months after the wedding, a son Howard was born, later to become a well-known poet. Diane was born March 14, 1923. (A third child, Renee, was born in October 1928.) The family was well off, with maids and a chauffeur and a nanny for each child. The nannies were totally in charge of the children, and the parents remained very distant. Their father was preoccupied with the store and showed little interest or warmth toward them, and this indifference lasted all his life. Their mother rose late, shopped a lot, and played cards with friends. Relationships between the parents and children were based on approval rather than love. As a young girl, visitors thought that Diane flirted with her father, and she admitted later in her life to having had incest fantasies about him. Diane was well aware of her father's philandering

---

[1]This section is based on Bosworth (1984).

in the 1930s, and her mother had a severe depression in 1938, perhaps exacerbated by her husband's infidelities.

Howard and Diane became inseparable. They were both very gifted. They read a lot and created rich fantasies together which they shared with no one else. Though they remained very close all their lives, they never discussed their work with each other and rarely mentioned each other to friends. When Renee, the third and final child was born, Diane showered her with affection and attention, perhaps affection which she had craved from her mother but never received.

When Diane was seven, she was sent to the Ethical Culture School on Central Park West, a private school based on the principles of Ethical Culture, a religious humanistic philosophy established by Felix Adler, a rabbi, in 1867. Diane was perceived as gifted there, but she later recalled that she felt quite dumb, a theme which characterised Diane all of her life. She was shy and had many childhood fears of monsters and kidnappers. One of her techniques for dealing with these fears was to stay in a dark room and wait for the monsters to come. The only external trauma was that she and Howard were robbed one day outside of their apartment building.

The family survived the Depression in reasonably good shape, and Diane was brought up like a well-bred eighteenth-century lady, acquiring the accomplishments of painting, piano, languages, manners and an appreciation of art. At school, her artistic creativity continued to develop. She became a leader and she was popular, floating from one clique to another yet remaining friends with all of them. However, she also liked to be by herself, reading poetry or looking at the art in the Metropolitan Museum of Art. Her father was proud of her artistic interests, and would sometimes take her along one weekend expeditions to museums and galleries. In 1935, he arranged for Diane to have sketching lessons after school from the illustrator for his stores.

Diana attended the Fieldston School from seventh through twelfth grade, a school which was a continuation of the Ethical Culture schools. The organization ran a settlement house in the slums which the students sometimes visited, and Diane was fascinated by the derelicts there. Diane and a friend would sometimes ride all over the city on the subways just to see the strange people who both frightened and pleased them. At fourteen, Diane was seen as shy and withdrawn, giving an impression of fragility. She spoke in rapid convulsive bursts with a soft voice, punctuated with giggles.

Allan Arbus was a nineteen year-old going to City College at night and working in the store's art department by day. His uncle was president of the company. Diane and he fell in love almost as soon as they met, and Diane, then fourteen, told her parents that she wanted to marry him. Her parents did everything they could to prevent this, but Diane and Allan continued to meet despite all of the obstacles.

By age fifteen, Diane was not wearing a bra or panty girdles. She disliked wearing elaborate dresses, did not shave her legs or wear make-up, and loved her menstrual flow. She masturbated a great deal, often in the bathroom window knowing that men in other apartments were watching her.

In July 1938, partly to break up Diane and Allan's romance, Diane's father sent her to the Cummington School of the Arts in Northampton, Massachusetts, for the summer. Diane spent most of the time there with Alex Eliot, the grandson of a Harvard University President, who fell in love with her. Allan visited, and the three became friends, a friendship which continued back in New York. Alex wanted to be a painter, Allan an actor. Alex noted that Allan treated Diane tenderly but dominatingly. (For example, he used to upbraid her for not finishing her sentences.)

Realising that Diane was attached to Allan, Alex attached himself to Ann Dicke, thirty years old, who had just broken off her engagement to the poet Robert Lowell. They married in 1940, and Diane and Anne became close friends too.

Diane's depressions were pronounced in her senior year, so much so that her teachers mentioned them to Howard, her brother, when he visited. When she graduated from high school, Diane gave no thought to going to college. She planned to marry Allan. Her parents gave in, finally, and Diane and Allan were married in a rabbi's chambers on April 19, 1941, one month after her eighteenth birthday. Her mother gave Diana a five year's supply of clothes from the family store and the services of a maid for a year. Diane and Allan could not afford a honeymoon, so they went to Boston and stayed with Alex and Anne. Alex and Anne moved soon afterwards to an apartment in Diane and Allan's building in New York City.

Fashion Photography

At first, Diane played the role of the good housewife, but the war interrupted their life. Allan joined the signal corps, and was sent to New Jersey and then to Queens to learn photography. Diane moved with him, and Allan would teach her in the evenings what he had learned during the days. Allan was sent to Burma in late 1944 and, after he left, Diane discovered she was pregnant. Their daughter, Doon, was born April 3, 1945.

Diane was living with her parents during this period and had fights with her mother about Doon. Her mother hired a nurse and wanted Doon bottle-fed. Diane wanted to breast-feed her. The compromise was that Diane would breast-feed Doon, after which the baby would be weighed to make sure she had gained enough.

When Allan came back from the war, he and Diane decided to be fashion photographers, a profession they had dabbled in back in 1941. After promising to buy all of their necessary photographic equipment and supplies, Diane's father reneged on his promise and gave them only a fraction of what they needed. However, he did give them their first job, photographing the store's fashions for newspaper ads. Observers of the scene noted that Diane and Allan worked very closely without any friction, unusual among collaborating couples in the city then. They were a shy, retiring couple, who did not join in the merrymaking in the evenings after fashion sessions and who seemed almost symbiotically close. People mistook them for brother and sister. Diane was slow-moving and dreamy, whereas Allan was brisk and organized, and they complemented each other in style. They both had spells of depression, Diane sitting dazedly in the apartment for hours, Allan playing his clarinet compulsively for hours. They continued to be inseparable from Alex and Anne Eliot.

However, by 1948 tensions were growing in the Eliot marriage. During a summer together at Martha's Vineyard, Alex who was now working for <u>Time</u>, read a chapter of possible novel to them all whereupon Anne exclaimed it was disgusting and horrible and left the island. Diane and Alex then became lovers. Anne was hospitalized, diagnosed with manic-depressive disorder, and she never forgave Diane. By 1950, Diane stopped sleeping with Alex, but they remained good friends. Alex then met and married Jane Winslow, and these two couples became close, though never as close as when Alex and Anne were married.

Diane and Allan were successful and were soon photographing for <u>Glamour</u> and other magazines, but they still found it hard to meet expenses. Diane's parents seemed proud of their success but never offered to help them financially. Diane sometimes asked directly for small cash sums from her father, which he would give to her. Diane's father continually criticized her appearance when Diane and Allan visited for the Sabbath supper. An uncle who had no children planned to leave his estate of four million dollars to Diane and her siblings, but Diane's father talked him out of it.

In 1951, Allan decided to take Diane and Doon to Europe for a year to have a break from the pressure of the work. After their return Diane became pregnant again and gave birth to Amy on April 16, 1954. Their career flourished, with work for <u>Glamour</u>, <u>Seventeen</u>, and <u>Vogue</u>, as well as for the leading advertising agencies. Yet Allan and Diane often complained about the "business," disliking the life involved in the profession. Contemporaries considered their fashion work excellent, but in the mold of the time. It was not creative or influential. At this time, Diane continued to photograph, but she was too shy to photograph strangers, so she photographed friends.

Diane's depressions seemed to be growing in frequency. They seemed unrelated to any specific incidents. Diane's biographer noted that both parents and all three children had recurrent depressions, suggesting a physiological and genetic basis, but Diane's depressions seemed longer and more severe. By 1956, Diane was telling her friends that she could not stand the fashion world much longer, and she began crying in public when their fashion work came up for discussion.

In 1957, Diane and Allan decided to stop working together. Allan would continue to do fashion work, but take lessons in mime. Diane would take up photography as an art form. Diane took lessons from Lisette Model at the New School. She was immediately drawn to the perverse, the alienated and the extreme. It took Diane a while to overcome her shyness in asking people to let her photograph them, but soon she was photographing circus freaks, deformed people, nudists, retardates, people during sex orgies and in bondage houses, and so on. She prowled the city at all hours looking for outcasts and strange people to photograph.

Meanwhile, Allan fell in love with a fellow actress, and in 1960 he and Diane separated. Allan pursued his acting career, but still did fashion photography work to support himself. He also continued to give money to Diane, keeping a joint account with her, and balancing their check book. Diane raised her two daughters, now aged six and fifteen, tried to obtain photography assignments, and worked on her projects.

At first, magazines rejected her portfolios, but in 1959 Diane found a mentor, Marvin Israel, a painter who had worked as an art director for magazines and who had contacts in the business. For the next eleven years, he advised and promoted Diane. Soon assignments arrived from Esquire, Harper's Bazaar, Show, The New York Times, New York magazine, and the British Sunday Times. She was awarded a Guggenheim fellowship in 1963 (on her third try) and a few years later in 1967 a second one, and soon Diane was selling most of the photographs she took. In 1965, three of her photographs were shown in the Museum of Modern Art. (One of the workers used to come in early to wipe the visitors' spit off Diane's photos. Two of the pictures were of nudists, and one of female impersonators.) In 1965, Diane taught a class at the Parson's School of Design. In 1967, the Museum of Modern art opened a large exhibition of Diane's work, perhaps the high point of her career. Although thrilled, she was also depressed by being on display. She began to worry about being imitated and changed the type of camera she used from time to time to prevent this. Yet she also continually denied her ability, doubting her skill. Her fame also made it seem harder to get magazine assignments and grants.

Last Years

Diane began to sleep with almost anyone, male or female, somewhat compulsively. Most of the sex was casual, but she also had a few longer relationships. She talked quite openly about her sexual encounters with friends, shocking them with the technicalities. However, her friends felt that she did not want or could not sustain a lasting love relationship.

Diane continued to have severe depressions. She had a therapist who prescribed antidepressants for her, "uppers." (She was not much of a drug user. She occasionally smoked marihuana, but she tried LSD only once.) In 1968, on her forty-fifth birthday, Diane began to express worries and fears about getting old. She began to wear make-up to hide her wrinkles.

Diane was ill with hepatitis briefly in 1966, and in 1968 the illness worsened. She was hospitalized and the hepatitis was diagnosed as the result of her use of antidepressants and birth control pills. She soon recovered. However, without the antidepressants, her emotions were closer to the surface and more open. She was irritated easily and cried often.

Diane's father died in 1963 of lung cancer and, by the end of the 1960s, her daughters were busy and often away. After the second bout of hepatitis, Diane was weak, talking to her friends on the telephone more (sometimes taping the calls and playing them back) and seeing them less. In 1968, Allan and Diane divorced, and Allan married Mariclaire Costello, a young actress, and moved to Hollywood. Diane was frightened at now truly being separated from Allan.

As her depressions worsened, doctors prescribed tranquilizers, but she was afraid to take them after the antidepressant-induced hepatitis. In the spring of 1969, she began to see a psychotherapist (a woman who followed Karen Horney's style of therapy). In 1970, Diane moved into Westbeth, a new artist's community near the Hudson River docks, and she seemed happier and less lonely. She was awarded the Robert Levitt Award from the American Society of Magazine Photographers, but she was still short of money, and to buy a $1000 camera she wanted she offered a private master class in photography. A friend tried to persuade her to consider a one person show at the Minneapolis Institute of Art. She was asked to teach a course at Yale University and to have her photographs in the Venice Biennale in 1972, but these offers provoked crying spells. She felt she did not deserve these honors. She denied that her work had any value.

Suicide was common among Diane's acquaintances. The off-Broadway director, Jess Kimmel, who lived in their building in 1958 killed himself, a friend Patti Greenfield fell to her death in 1967. In 1963, Diane discussed suicide intellectually with a friend. She was fascinated by the details of suicide, such as the hesitation cuts made by wrist-slashers, and she said that she would like to have photographed the faces of Marilyn Monroe and Ernest Hemingway in death. In 1971, two people jumped from the roof of the Westbeth building in which Diane lived. In the summer of 1971, Diane helped Marvin Israel on a small sculpture of a person who had slashed his wrists.

The summer of 1971 was typically hot and humid, and many of Diane's friends had left the city for the summer, as she and Allan used to do. She made increasingly frequent allusions to suicide and how she could not go on much longer. She killed herself in her apartment on July 26. She was found two days later, lying in an empty bathtub with her wrists slit, but the medical examiner found that the death was caused by acute barbiturate poisoning.

Discussion

Diane's life has several noteworthy aspects. The family history of depression suggests, of course, a genetically-transmitted affective disorder. But Diane's depressions seemed worse than those of the other family members.

Diane seems to have mastered her depressions early in life by falling in love and marrying early. The breakup of her marriage produced a major change in her life, a move into creative photography with its attendant anxieties over financial survival and artistic worth. Diane seems never to have felt secure about her talent, and her successes did little to allay this insecurity.

The loss of Allan also led to a frenetic search for companionship, including compulsive casual sex and a hectic round of friendship. But this excessive activity indicates that the good relationship (with Allan) had helped to hold her together and keep her functioning. After the breakup, she never found a replacement. Marvin Israel might have made a good replacement, but he was contentedly married.

Diane entered her mid-life crisis then with artistic insecurity and loneliness. Despite reaching the pinnacle of success, she felt that she had nothing to look forward to except loneliness, old age and disease, a waning of her talents, and continuing intense depressions. For Diane, suicide seemed to be the only alternative.

Sylvia Plath

Sylvia Plath was an American poet who died at the age of thirty in 1963 in England by putting her head in the gas oven. Today, she might not have died in this way because during the 1960s the British detoxified domestic gas, removing the carbon monoxide from it, and eventually switching to natural gas which contains no carbon monoxide (Clarke and Lester, 1989). But Sylvia Plath had already died and, even if she could not have used gas, she might have switched to another method, such as the medications she used in an earlier attempt when she was twenty one.

What brought Sylvia to this crisis? For the details of her life, I have relied on the biography by Butscher (1976).

Her Parents

Sylvia's father, Otto Plath, was born in 1885 in the German town of Grabow. He emigrated to the United States when he was fifteen to join his father in North Dakota. After college, he pursued his interest in entomology, going to Harvard in his 30s to study for his doctorate, leaving his first wife behind in Oregon. Otto got his doctorate in 1928, at the age of forty three, specializing in the study of bees. He began teaching at Boston University where he met a student called Aurelia Schober, twenty one years his junior.

Aurelia was born in Boston to Roman Catholic parents who were from Austria. Early in 1932, Otto and Aurelia travelled to Nevada so that Otto could divorce his first wife and marry Aurelia. They set up house in Jamaica Plain, near the university and near the Arboretum where Otto conducted his research.

Sylvia was born on October 27, 1932. She was somewhat frail because of a sinus condition that plagued her for the rest of her life. Two and a half years later, her brother Warren was born.

Early Years

The family bought a house in Winthrop in 1937, near the sea and Aurelia's parents. The early years were uneventful. Sylvia apparently was quite bright and used her intelligence to please her father, as many first-borns do. She learnt the Latin names for insects, and Otto would show off her skill to visitors. From the beginning, she earned straight A's in school, impressing teachers with her intelligence and dedication.

Otto was diabetic and neglected his condition. His leg became gangrenous and was amputated, and the complications of bronchopneumonia killed him on November 5, 1940, eight days after Sylvia's birthday. Aurelia left both children at home during the funeral, which Sylvia eventually listed as one of her grievances against her mother.

The family was now in financial difficulty. Aurelia took a teaching position at Boston University's school for secretarial studies and had her parents and brother move in with her to share expenses. Eventually, she decided to move to Wellesley where she could raise her children in an educated and middle class community and help Sylvia's sinus condition and Warren's asthma. Thereafter, Aurelia strove to give her children high achievement experiences. In addition to school, she provided extracurricular activities in scouting, sailing, piano and viola lessons, dancing, painting and summer camps.

Sylvia's first poem appeared in the Boston Sunday Herald when she was eight and a half, and she won a prize with a drawing in another contest. As she progressed through school, her work continued to be outstanding, receiving many awards. She quickly developed an interest in literature and in writing. At junior high school she received straight A's and a perfect record of punctuality. Her poems and drawings continued to win prizes. Her IQ was about 160. Socially she was a bit of a loner, though she had many good friends, she did not date much, and she spent long hours studying, reading and writing.

High school continued in the same vein. She took the advanced literature courses and edited the school magazine in her senior year. Her stories and poems appeared in magazines such as <u>Seventeen</u> and the <u>Christian Science Monitor</u>. She was also active in the local Unitarian church and the community. She was admitted to Smith College and awarded a scholarship.

Her menstruation began with cramps and an irregular and copious flow. She did not date much until her senior year. But this was 1950 when sexual behavior was quite inhibited and heavy petting as far as people went.

Her biographer does not mention much at all about psychological problems at this time in Sylvia's life. Knowing that she eventually killed herself, Butscher sees all kinds of portents of this later fate, but the only symptoms he mentions are severe depressions whenever her sinuses or menstrual cramps bothered her. The frequency and severity of the depressions is unclear.

Smith College and the First Suicide Attempt

Sylvia's career at Smith was outstanding. From the first, she obtained A's, and her literary achievements steadily grew. She made many friends there, some staying close to her for the rest of her life. It was considered crucial at Smith to date and to date the right kind of men. Since Sylvia had no relationships with appropriate men from her school days, she went on many blind dates, until a friend from high school days, the Buddy Willard of her novel <u>The Bell Jar</u>, took her to the Yale senior prom. Thereafter, Sylvia managed always to have a 'boy friend' available. Her relationship with Buddy had some friction, and eventually other boy-friends would come along. But her biographer, Butscher, feels that Sylvia saw marriage as an inevitable and desirable goal and needed always to have a man in her life who could be viewed as a potential husband. Periods of unattachment were hard for her. Buddy was admitted to Harvard Medical School but had to drop out with tuberculosis. Sylvia wrote to him and maintained the illusion that he was her boyfriend, but she gradually began to get involved with others.

Sylvia's stay at Smith was, of course, the first separation from her mother. Aurelia used to write to Sylvia every day, which suggests that the separation was harder on Aurelia than on Sylvia. In addition, the status of being a scholarship student did carry an inferior status in those days. But there were few other traumas for Sylvia.

Her scholarship patron was a popular novelist, Mrs. Olive Prouty (Higgins), and Sylvia was encouraged by the college to keep in contact with her. This relationship proved to be useful to Sylvia later during her breakdown. When Sylvia decided that a successful college career involved extracurricular activities, she participated in all kinds, successfully building up a record of involvement.

In summers at Wellesley Sylvia had worked, and she also found work at Smith. Her first summer was spent working as a mother's helper for a family in Swampscott, an exclusive resort on the coast, and her second summer as a waitress and mother's helper.

In her junior year she broke-up with Buddy, but he had already been replaced by Myron Lotz. She broke her leg while skiing during the Christmas recess, but this did not impede her college work. The year ended with Sylvia winning a position as guest editor for Mademoiselle for June.

This is the summer of 1953 which is the focus of Sylvia's later novel The Bell Jar, written mostly during 1961 and 1962. For this month, Sylvia worked for Cyrilly Abels, reading and judging manuscripts, and participating in all of the social activities planned for the group of guest editors. Abels noticed Sylvia's distancing manner and tried to break through and relate to the real Sylvia, but she failed to penetrate Sylvia's social mask.

Back in Wellesley, Sylvia was rejected for a course on creative writing at Harvard summer school which left her with two months to fill. She fell into an increasingly severe depression. Aurelia eventually became concerned enough to take her to a local psychiatrist, the 'Dr. Gordon' of the novel, who after a few sessions of psychotherapy recommended electroconvulsive therapy at his clinic. (We must also remember that in the 1950s, effective anti-depressant medications had not yet been developed.)

The idea of suicide grew. She contemplated using a razor blade and drowning. But eventually, on a Monday morning in August, she took forty-eight sleeping pills from where her mother had locked them up, went into the basement of the house after leaving a note saying that she was going for a hike and would be back the next day, and crawled behind some wood that was stacked there. Her mother called the police that evening, and search parties were organized. But Sylvia was not found until Wednesday afternoon when her grandmother went into the basement to do the laundry and heard Sylvia moaning.

After a week in the hospital, Sylvia was transferred to the locked psychiatric ward at Massachusetts General Hospital. Sylvia's patron at Smith College, Mrs. Prouty, paid for her to be transferred to McLean's Hospital. There Sylvia received insulin shock therapy at first and then electroshock therapy again, but this was supplemented by psychotherapy from a female psychiatrist, the Dr. Jones of The Bell Jar. She was released just before Christmas 1953.

Sylvia spent another year and a half at Smith, graduating in June 1955. This period saw a more extraverted Sylvia, one who now also took pains to be beautiful and fashionably dressed, still the campus literary star and with a romantic aura from being an attempted suicide. Her virginity was lost (and she developed the reputation of being rather loose).[2] There were minor upsets, such as the rejection by Myron Lotz, whom Sylvia had seen as a potential husband. She continued to see Dr. Jones occasionally.

In the summer of 1954, Sylvia was accepted at summer school at Harvard University to study German. It was there she met Edwin, a married man with a wife in St Louis where he was a professor, who may or may not have raped her. However, her night with him precipitated severe hemorrhaging.

Sylvia quieted down a little in her senior year and worked hard at her studies. She was awarded a Fulbright scholarship upon graduation in 1955 and decided to go to Cambridge University in England to study.

Cambridge University and Ted Hughes

Sylvia spent two years at Cambridge University, at Newnham College, where she eventually obtained her second BA. Her stay there was filled with course work, writing, and dating. At Christmas, she visited France and a former lover who was now there. But in February 1956, she met Ted Hughes whom she would soon marry.

Ted, an aspiring poet and writer like Sylvia, had graduated from Cambridge in 1954 and had worked in various odd jobs. He was now living in London. Sylvia planned to visit Germany in the Spring where her current 'potential husband' was living, but they argued and broke off their relationship. Sylvia also saw her ex-lover in France for the last time. On her return to England in April 1956, Sylvia and Ted got engaged. [3] They married in June, with Sylvia's mother in attendance, and went to Spain for their honeymoon.

Their first year of marriage was made difficult by the fact that undergraduates could not marry without permission at Cambridge University. Eventually, Sylvia was pardoned and moved out from Newnham College into an apartment with Ted. Sylvia's Fulbright award was renewed, and Ted got a teaching job at a boy's secondary school.

Sylvia began to work with dedication on their literary careers, typing up and sending off submissions of both her work and Ted's. Their publications grew more and more numerous, and Ted had his first collection of poems accepted for publication in 1957.

---

[2] On a boat trip to England in 1955, the joke was that Sylvia never got a decent meal because she was always sleeping with someone! Butscher notes that Sylvia remained faithful to her husband, Ted Hughes, and so her quest for lovers ended with her marriage.

[3] Sylvia's grandmother died from cancer that April after a painful illness.

They decided to move to the United States in 1957, and Sylvia got a teaching job at Smith College. Ted remained unemployed till 1958 when he got a teaching job at the University of Massachusetts. Sylvia found that an instructor's position teaching freshman English left little time for writing, and so she decided to quit teaching at the end of the year in 1958.

The marriage seemed quite happy. In these initial phases, Ted was the more successful poet. He soon had a second book of poems completed and a book of children's stories. His poems appeared in The New Yorker. They decided to return to England, especially as Ted was not happy in the United States. But first they spent a year in Boston, supported by Sylvia working at odd jobs for a while and then by a Guggenheim fellowship won by Ted. They were trying to have children (though Sylvia was more motivated to have a family than was Ted) and sought medical advice when conception did not occur soon enough. They spent three months touring the United States during the summer of 1959, and during this trip Sylvia became pregnant.

After a stay at Yaddoo, the artists' colony near Saratoga Springs in New York, Sylvia and Ted left for England in December 1959. Sylvia was twenty-seven, pregnant, and headed for permanent residence in a foreign country.

England and the End

They first rented an apartment in London. Sylvia gave birth to Frieda in April 1960 and, after a miscarriage in February 1961 to a son Nicholas in January 1962. [4] Their literary careers continued to progress, and Sylvia had her first book of poems published in 1960. They won prize after prize and by 1961 were successful enough as writers that their finances were thereafter in good shape. In 1961, Sylvia was awarded a Saxton Foundation grant to work on The Bell Jar.

In 1961, they bought a house in Croton, Devon, with the help of loans from both of their families. Life was full and busy with writing and the children and a new house to fix up, yet Butscher describes Sylvia in early 1962 as tense and tired and subject to fits of depression. Visitors, however, saw no marital trouble and viewed the life there as 'idyllic'.

Butscher says little about Ted. Perhaps Ted was not enthusiastic about having children? Perhaps after being the more successful writer in the family at first, he was threatened by Sylvia's growing skill and success? But he had had his way in the decision to move back to England and to live in Devon. However, by the summer of 1962 another woman had entered his life.

Butscher calls her Olga, married to a Canadian poet (after a failed first marriage). Olga seems to have pursued Ted, flirting with him even in

---

[4] The miscarrage was followed three weeks later by acute appendicitis.

his own home in Croton. But he too fell in love with her. The affair was in earnest by the summer of 1962. (Olga appears to have quite unstable herself, later identifying with Sylvia and believing herself to be almost Sylvia's reincarnation. She later committed suicide with gas, killing her young daughter too, possibly Ted's child though Butscher is not explicit about this.)

In August, Olga telephoned Ted, trying to disguise her voice. Sylvia ripped the telephone off the wall and fled to friends.[5] She returned the next day and asked Ted to leave as soon as her mother had departed for the United States. Sylvia kept hoping that Ted would come back to her. She came down with a severe bout of influenza, and Ted did come back to help out. In September, Sylvia thought she and Ted were to have a holiday together in Ireland, but Ted left her after one day for Olga in London.

Her thirtieth birthday came in October 1962, with Sylvia alone in Devon with two children, deserted by her husband, writing poems furiously every morning. Sylvia decided to find an apartment in London and rent the house in Devon to others. She moved in the middle of December.

Sylvia was safe financially, though, of course, she worried a lot about money. However, in London she found that many of 'their' friends were now 'his' friends. Both she and Ted also worked for the BBC which was sometimes awkward. Sylvia was alone with the children that Christmas. Ted visited the children regularly, but these meetings were hard on Sylvia.

The last few weeks of her life were difficult. She had corrected the galley proofs for <u>The Bell Jar</u> and was awaiting publication and comment. She was working feverishly, smoking heavily, hardly sleeping and eating little. She had lost twenty pounds since the summer. She had influenza, after which the children came down with it. The winter was one of the worst ever, with frozen plumbing, strikes by the electrical workers, and snow and ice everywhere. Sylvia endured a bathtub that would not empty and dripping pipes in the ceiling. The weather did not break until the end of January.

The reviews of her book appeared at the end of January, and they were lukewarm. (She had published it under a pseudonym which meant that reviewers would be less likely to give the work close attention and praise the Sylvia Plath whom they knew.) Her recent poems were being rejected.

Sylvia had plans for the future though. The Devon house was to be rented to an Australian couple, and she was to return there in the summer. Nicholas needed treatment for his eye, and Frieda was enrolled in a nursery school.

In the last week of her life, from February 4th 1963 to February 11th, Sylvia had a fever and wild fluctuations in her moods. She had lost

---

[5] Sylvia's mother was staying with them at this time.

her au pair girl and the weather was still bad. Her physician recognized her depression and had arranged for Sylvia to see a therapist (whose letter to her was delivered to the wrong address). By Friday the 8th he had tried to get three clinics to admit her, but all refused. He arranged for a nurse to come on Monday morning. Sylvia went away for the weekend to visit friends, returning on Sunday evening.

At 6am on Monday February 11th, Sylvia took milk and bread up to the children's rooms and went to the kitchen where she sealed the door. She put her head in the gas oven and was found there later in the morning when the nurse finally broke in with the aid of some workmen.

Discussion

The loss of her father when she was eight looms large as a factor in Sylvia's life, especially because of the way she wrote about him. However, after reading of her anger toward him in her novel and poems, it is a shock to find that he was a mild mannered academic, the age of a grandfather more than a father, who died of natural causes. His greatest fault seems to be that he spent too much time with his bees and his research.

Nonetheless, Sylvia was full of anger for his rejection of her, both while he was alive and in his death. Her poem written in the months prior to her suicide casts him as a devil, a concentration camp guard with her as a victim. She sees Ted as a father substitute. And yet she loves her father too and casts her suicide attempt years earlier as an attempt to be reunited with him. (Interestingly, Sylvia eventually kept bees, as did her father, and she studied German the language of her father. Her identification with him was strong.)

Though her depressions are not documented well at all, it is likely that she had an affective disorder (a psychotic depression). She had her first breakdown as an undergraduate, and she lived in fear that it would occur again. Might her suicide have been motivated in part also by a fear of becoming psychotic again?

On top of this, there is the loss of her husband, whom she loved, and who provided her with the environment to flourish as a mother and author. He rejected her for another. (Interestingly, Sylvia was upset in her marriage by the very close relationship between Ted and his sister Olwyn, which she saw as incestuous. In a memorable row when Sylvia was eight months pregnant with Nicholas, Olwyn told Sylvia how much she resented Sylvia. Ted did not take Sylvia's side at all in this, which hurt her deeply.)

In her novel about her psychiatric breakdown in 1953, Sylvia shows a distrust of her ability. She had worked hard to get good grades and to publish, but she feared that the success was temporary. Curiously enough though, Sylvia was quite resilient in her writing career, sending off poems and stories despite rejections.

Butscher makes much of the facade Sylvia put on. Sylvia seems, more than the average person, to have suppressed the real Sylvia, assuming a mask that would gain approval from others. Good grades (reinforced by her father's admiration for her academic skills), desirable boy friends (and eventually lovers), and awards and honors all served to bolster her self-esteem. But eventually you have to come to like yourself for what you are, regardless of the reactions of others, and this perhaps comes in middle age, too late for Sylvia.

There are few other symptoms to be noted about Sylvia. A possessiveness about her belongings, especially her books. Her chronic sinus condition. Nothing more.

Thus, her suicide makes sense only in the light of a chronic depressive condition, a condition that colored her world view and made the loss of her father so much harder to adjust to. Then, at the peak of her creative life but hopeless, she chose to leave the living, her children, and return to the dead, her father.

Anne Sexton

Anne Sexton was born as Anne Harvey on November 9, 1928, in Newton, Massachusetts. She was the third of three daughters. Her father, Ralph, born in 1900, worked in the wool business and eventually established his own firm, and his father was a banker who suffered a psychiatric breakdown under the stress of his business. Anne's father had a younger sister who attempted suicide in her twenties and eventually shot herself to death in 1975 (Middlebrook, 1991).

Anne's mother, Mary Gray, born in 1901, was the only child of the editor and publisher of the Lewiston Evening Journal. After her junior year at Wellesley College, she met Ralph Harvey and quit college to marry him.

Of the three children, the eldest, Jane, became Daddy's girl, and she committed suicide in 1983 with sleeping pills. Blanche was seen as the clever child, while Anne was the baby of the family. A nurse helped with the family, and she stayed until Ralph Harvey's death, becoming like an aunt to the three girls. The parents were very close, and the children used to think up ways to gain their parents' attention such as writing them notes or leaving drawings on their parents' pillows.

Anne's father drank heavily, and when drunk he was often irascible. In particular, he used to insult Anne, saying for example that her acne disgusted him and that he could not eat his food with her at the table. Later, in therapy, Anne said that her father sexually molested her. However, her therapist (Martin Orne) noted that her account varied each time she recalled it, and he concluded that it probably had not happened. Orne suggested that the incident was a metaphor for Anne's experience of her father during this period. Anne's mother also drank, but regarded herself as a drunk rather than an alcoholic like her husband. Ralph Harvey finally sought treatment and gave up drinking in 1950.

When Anne was eleven, she was hospitalized for constipation, and her mother showed great anxiety over Anne's bowel movements, threatening her with a colostomy if she was not regular. Her father's aunt, Nana, moved in at this time, and Anne spent almost all of her spare time with Nana. However, after a couple of years, Nana suddenly lost her hearing and became quite child-like in her behavior. After some episodes of violence, Nana was given electroconvulsive therapy at a psychiatric hospital and eventually placed in a clinic. Around this time too, Anne's paternal grandfather had his second breakdown and was hospitalized. Later Anne came to think that maybe she had caused Nana's breakdown and that one day she would break down too.

In junior high school, Anne had many friends and began to take an interest in her appearance. Anne had a steady boy friend, Jack, from eighth grade into high school, and even at sixteen Anne and her friends went to bars and dances. Their favorite drink was Singapore slings. To calm Anne down, her parents sent her to girl's boarding school. Nevertheless, Anne got engaged to Jack, but he broke off the engagement soon afterwards, leaving Anne heartbroken. Anne's time at high school was full of activities - swimming, basketball, cheerleading, theater and poetry. Her father liked her poems but always told Anne that she was not as brilliant as her mother. Anne's mother was jealous of her daughter, and her attitude led Anne to stop writing for ten years.

After the private high school, Anne went to the Garland School in Boston. She quickly became engaged again, but in the summer she met Alfred Sexton, known as Kayo, fell in love with him, slept with him, broke her engagement, and, thinking that she was pregnant and with the consent of her mother, eloped to get married in North Carolina in August, 1948. Kayo went back to Colgate University where he was an undergraduate, but he dropped out at Thanksgiving, and the Sextons moved in with Kayo's parents. Kayo got a job in the wool business, while Anne did some modelling. They found an apartment in Cochituate (Massachusetts), and soon Anne fell in love with husband of a couple with whom they were friendly. Nothing developed from this, but Anne did consider divorce at the time and took an overdose of sleeping pills while others were around who could save her. Her mother suggested she seek counseling with Dr. Martha Brunner-Orne, the psychiatrist who had treated Anne's father for alcoholism.

At the start of the Korean War in 1950, Kayo joined the naval reserve and was shipped overseas. Anne soon began dating other men, but her mother found out and persuaded Anne to join Kayo in San Francisco. Once there, she became pregnant and came back to Massachusetts to give birth. Linda was born July 21, 1953. Kayo returned three days later to take up civilian life again. He joined Ralph Harvey's business as a road salesman. A second daughter, Joy, was born August 4, 1955.

Anne felt very constrained by the geographic closeness of her parents and her in-laws and by having Kayo work for her father. Anne was sensitive to the criticism from both sets of parents, and she and Kayo dreamed of leaving the area but never did.

Psychiatric Problems

Soon after the birth of Joy, Anne had what appears to be a postpartum depression. She consulted with Dr. Brunner-Orne who gave her medications and counseling. A few months later, Anne began to fear that she might harm the children. She suffered anxiety attacks, especially when Kayo was away on business, and was physically abusive to her daughters.

Eventually, Dr. Brunner-Orne recommended hospitalization at a private clinic. Anne was released in August, 1956, after a stay of three weeks. It was decided that Anne would see Dr. Brunner-Orne's son for psychotherapy, and Anne saw Dr. Martin Orne for the next eight years. Linda, now three, went to stay with Anne's sister, Blanche, for five months. Joy went to stay with Anne's mother-in-law, Billie, for the next three years.

Anne did not improve quickly. In November, she overdosed with barbiturates during Kayo's absence but called Billie to recuse her. Orne put her in a psychiatric hospital for five weeks, and Anne called this a psychotic breakdown and thought that she was possibly insane. Orne, then and later, did not consider Anne psychotic. He eventually diagnosed her as an hysteric neurotic. One problem in therapy was that Anne forgot much of what transpired in each session, and she seemed to have a tendency to fall into "trances" easily. Eventually Orne had her make notes after sessions and listen to tapes of the sessions.

Early in treatment, Orne suggested that Anne write about her experiences in treatment, and Anne began to write poetry again. After another suicide attempt in May 1957 (following her mother's mastectomy for cancer which her mother blamed on the stress created by Anne), Orne forcefully argued that her poems might help others who had similar problems, and Anne began to seriously consider poetry as a vocation. In 1957, she brought over sixty poems to Orne for him to read. She decided then to enroll in a poetry workshop held at the Boston Center for Adult Education taught by John Holmes, a professor at Tufts University (whose first wife had committed suicide). Anne, timid at first, soon felt at home there and stayed two years. Her first poem was published in a local magazine in April, 1958. Thereafter, with surprising persistence, Anne submitted her poems for publication, recording the rejections, but never giving up.

Anne requested a third meeting each week with Orne, and he agreed provided that she paid for it (instead of letting her father-in-law pay). Anne did so by getting a of selling cosmetics door-to-door. Billie was now even more involved with Anne's life, taking care of Anne's family whenever Anne was too upset to do so.

Anne met a fellow writer, Maxine Kumin, at the poetry workshop, and they soon became close friends, calling each other every day to discuss their writing. They went to poetry readings together and socialized with their families. Anne also soon found a lover among her classmates.

By mid-1958, Anne had sixty poems in circulation, seeking publication, and the <u>Christian Science Monitor</u> accepted two for their July issues. Soon she had acceptances from the <u>Antioch Review</u>, <u>Harper's</u>, and <u>The New Yorker</u>. Anne was now taking antidepressants, and Joy came home for longer and longer periods. But at the same time, Kayo became increasingly upset by Anne's devotion to her poetry and her accompanying neglect of her family. The arguments often turned into physical fights, followed by remorse on Kayo's part. Anne eventually came to see that she wanted the physical attacks in part as punishment for her poor behavior. (In 1960 at Anne's insistence, Kayo went into psychotherapy for almost two years and got his anger under better control for a while.) Later that year (1958), Anne's father had a stroke, and her mother's cancer metastasized. In November, Anne went to her therapist's clinic for several days.

Anne went off to Ohio for a one-week poetry conference where she met W. D. Snodgrass with whom Anne corresponded for a year. In September, 1958, Anne joined Robert Lowell's poetry class at Boston University. At the end of 1958, the <u>Hudson Review</u> accepted a 240-line poem, and Anne began planning her first book. Anne showed great professionalism as a poet. She worked hard on redrafting poems, courting the editors of journals, and publishing poems separately in journals before they appeared in book form - in short, actively promoting herself. She also began to develop a public image which led to her becoming one of the most memorable performers on the poetry circuit.

The Mature Poet

Anne's life pattern now crystalized into several themes. First, she continued to write productively and receive acclaim for her work. Poems and books appeared regularly, and prizes and honors were awarded to her, including a fellowship at the Radcliffe Institute, the Levinson prize from <u>Poetry</u> in 1962, a traveling fellowship from the American Academy of Arts and Letters in 1963 (for which she went to Europe with a female companion in 1963 and with Kayo in 1964), a travel grant from the International Congress of Cultural Freedom in 1964 (for which she took Kayo on a safari to Kenya), a fellowship from Royal Society of Literature in 1964, the Shelley Memorial Prize from the Poetry Society of America and a Pulitzer Prize in 1967, a Guggenheim Foundation grant in 1969, an honorary doctorate from Tufts University in 1970, and a visiting professorship at Colgate University in 1972. Her poetry readings increased in popularity until she was demanding $1000 for each reading.

Not all was successful. Anne tried to publish short stories and a novel, but failed in this. She tried several plays, but only one was performed, Mercy Street in 1968 (though she was more successful with a musical ensemble which set her poetry readings to music). In addition, the British reception for her poetry and her readings was nowhere near as positive as the American response.

Anne became poet in residence at a public high school in 1967 and the next year led a writing workshop at McLean's Hospital. In 1970, she began teaching part-time at Boston University and did so for the remainder of her life. Though she read at a few anti-Vietnam War rallies, Anne stayed uninvolved with the social and political issues of the day.

Writing continued to dominate her life, and she neglected chores, so that Kayo and her daughters, as well as her mother-in-law, all helped keep the household running while Anne wrote, traveled or stayed in psychiatric clinics. Eventually Anne's self-centeredness led her to parentalize her daughters so that they had to take care of her, and she used them for her comfort even to the point of sexually molesting them. She slept with and masturbated while lying in bed with Linda when Linda was eleven, and she kissed and masturbated by rubbing against Linda when Linda was fifteen, after which Linda began psychotherapy.

Anne continued to take lovers to the point that her behavior seems promiscuous since none of them developed into an alternative relationship for that with Kayo. In 1960, she had an abortion because she was not certain that the child was Kayo's. She also had a brief homosexual encounter with a friend in 1965.

By 1966, Joy was also in psychotherapy, and Anne was thinking of divorcing Kayo. Anne realized that she was dependent upon Kayo for her stable home life, but she also resented his lack of support for her career as a poet. By 1969, Kayo was becoming violent again. His wife was brazen about her affairs, talking to lovers on the telephone when Kayo was home, and they were drunk by dinner-time most evenings. She moved out in January, 1973, but, after a court hearing in March, Kayo moved out of their house, leaving it to Anne. Anne found a live-in couple to help with the household, but they fled from her after a few months. Her daughters were growing up and away from her, and Anne found fewer available men for lovers.

Although Anne had developed a public persona which was witty and extraverted, she was tremendously insecure about meeting others and suffered great anxiety before public talks and parties. Eventually, she took to drinking alcohol to calm herself before public appearances. However, soon after her breakdown in the early 1950s, Anne had panicked whenever she had to leave the house, and so her development as a poet certainly reduced the level of her anxiety. Anne liked to have someone with her when she went to sleep, Kayo or some lover, even after she started taking sleeping pills regularly which knocked her out in minutes. One lover described her taking an indiscriminate mix of major and minor tranquilizers, antidepressants and barbiturates before bedtime. By the 1970s, Anne was clearly abusing both alcohol and medications.

Anne needed, and was lucky to have, a series of colleagues or mentors, other poets, with whom she would correspond voluminously about work, as well as close-neighbors like Maxine Kumin and, later, Lois Ames with whom to share ideas and trips. After she fell and broke her hip in 1966, a neighbor, Joan Smith, helped nurse Anne and continued to help Anne for the rest of her life.

She continued to attempt suicide, seek frequent stays at clinics (which she also used as writing retreats), and to remain in psychotherapy. In 1974, after seven years of working with Anne, Orne moved to Philadelphia, and he was replaced by a therapist who committed professional misconduct by becoming Anne's lover. (He rejected Anne as a lover later when his wife found out about the affair.) When this therapeutic relationship ended in 1969, Anne transferred to a third therapist, this time a women, who demanded that Anne break off her occasional sessions with Orne whenever he returned to Boston. In late 1973, this third therapist, angered at Anne, ended the relationship. Anne began to visit a social worker until a replacement therapist could be found, but in October 1974 she committed suicide.

In 1964, after a severe breakdown, Anne stayed in Massachusetts General Hospital, where she was given an antidepressant (imipramine) but switched to a phenothiazine (Thorazine). She took this for the rest of her life, but she felt that it destroyed her creativity (and prevented her from sunbathing), and so she often went for periods without taking it so that she could write. However, during those periods she would then become quite manic.

Suicide continued to fascinate Anne. She attempted suicide many times herself and for many years carried barbiturates in her purse with everywhere in case the mood to die came on her suddenly. She talked to Sylvia Plath in the late Fifties about their earlier suicide attempts, and she was moved by Plath's suicide in 1963. A friend, Ruth Soter, possibly killed herself in 1964.

Anne suffered several losses in adulthood. Her mother died in March, 1959, and her father in June, 1959. Her father-in-law was killed in a car crash in 1960. Her sister-in-law was killed in a car accident on her honeymoon in 1969. But most important of all, in 1970, she met a man who claimed to be her real father and persuaded Anne that his affair with her mother had indeed resulted in Anne's conception. Anne's psychological state deteriorated after this disclosure - the first suicide attempt since 1966 and the first clinic stay since 1964.

The End

By the end of 1973, Anne was divorced but regretting it. She was living alone, abusing alcohol and drugs, having difficulty writing, and deserted by her friends who were bored by her problems and who disliked her drunken behavior. She took to phoning friends at all hours. In late 1973, her therapist refused to continue in therapy with her, and she began seeing a social worker for counseling. In December 1973, Philip Rahv, an old friend, committed suicide. Anne made two suicide attempts with medications in September, 1973, and two more over the Winter, but she told a friend that car exhaust was the way to die. Sexually deprived, she put personal ads in the local newspaper. She also took religious instruction and contemplated being baptized as an Episcopalian. Nothing seemed to work or to help her. On October 4th, she went into her garage, turned the radio on and started the car. She was soon dead.

Discussion

For Anne Sexton, suicide was almost a way of life. A rough listing of her attempts (all with medications) is 1949, November 1956, May 1957, November 1961, July 1966, August 1970, September 1973 (two), Winter 1973-1974 (two), February 1974, and Spring 1974. Interestingly, she switched methods for her final successful suicidal act.

Anne remained in psychotherapy from 1956 until her death in 1974, and she was hospitalized on many occasions (at least seven times between 1956 and 1964 and at least four more times between 1971 and 1974). She took antidepressants and Thorazine (and suffered from some of the side effects, including tardive dyskinesia), but never received electroconvulsive therapy.

Anne fits well with her first therapist's diagnosis of hysteric. She was critically dependent upon attention, succor and love from others. Alone, she panicked and fell into depressions. Like some of R. D. Laing's cases (Laing, 1960), Anne seemed to exist only when there were others to notice her. Her promiscuity fits well into this pattern. Her decision to divorce Kayo, coming as it did with her daughters' growing independence and her mother-in-law's remarriage, was perhaps a mistake. Although her final decline began some time before the divorce, it increased afterwards.

Anne was in psychotherapy from 1956 to 1974, and it is remarkable that it failed to save her or even modify her behavior much at all. Anne was depressed, a substance abuser, promiscuous and prone to trances right to the end. The therapist misconduct is also striking. One therapist used her for sexual intercourse; another demanded that she break with her first therapist (Orne) and then eventually abandoned her.

Her first therapist, Orne, seems to have hit upon the right vocation for Anne in encouraging her to write poetry, much of which was based on her experiences as a psychiatric patient. Anne, along with Robert Lowell and Sylvia Plath, encouraged poets to deal with subject matter long avoided, such as madness and the everyday concerns of normal people, including pregnancy and menstruation. It has been argued that writing poetry enabled Anne to survive longer than she might otherwise have done (Lester and Terry, 1992).

However, Anne remained developmentally immature, perhaps hampered by her parents ignoring her, except for harsh criticism, and her father's drunkenness and abuse. She never grew into a mature person, capable of taking care of herself or others, preferring the role of a dependent child. Finally, having rejected some and having been abandoned by others, she killed herself. Without the attention of others, Anne did not feel as if she really existed. Left alone, death could hardly be worse.

Sara Teasdale

Sara Teasdale was born on August 8, 1884 in St. Louis, Missouri. She was the fourth born, with a brother George aged twenty, a sister Mary (Mamie) seventeen, and a brother John fourteen. She was christened Sarah Trevor Teasdale, but later dropped the final "h". At home she was known as Sadie.[6]

Sara's father had intended to study law but went into business at the age of seventeen after his father died suddenly. He had been successful, ending up as a wholesaler in dried fruits, beans and nuts. He met his wife at the Third Baptist Church, where they were married in 1863, and they remained devoutly religious. At Sara's birth, her mother was forty and her father forty-five. Sara was almost like a grandchild in the family, only five years older than the first grandchild.

The dominant parent was her mother. Like her daughter, she too had a sickly childhood but became transformed upon marriage. Now she was an energetic and domineering mother. Sara's biographer speculates that to have had a daughter at the age of forty was unseemly in Victorian times. It advertised the fact that she and her husband still engaged in sexual intercourse. Her determination to bring her daughter up as the model of gentility was possibly an attempt to compensate for this shadow on her virtue.

Sara was watched over anxiously from birth and had an early tendency to frailness. She was never strong, got colds easily and was

---

[6] This section is based on Drake (1979).

easily exhausted. When she caught a cold, she was treated as if she had pneumonia and put to bed. For much of her life, her family hired a nurse to be with her to ease the burden of daily tasks and see that Sara did not overtax her strength. Drake suggested that this concern for her led to Sara's life-long anxiety about her health. Her mother crippled Sara by her kindness and lavish concern. Sara's sickliness was not a cause of her lack of energy; rather it was a result of Sara trying to suppress her energy.

Sara was not exceptionally beautiful, and she always regretted this. She was indulged, surrounded by luxuries, given whatever she needed, and excused from household responsibilities. Sara never cooked, mended, or cleaned house. Sara was a placid, sweet-tempered and obedient child who learned to inhibit her hostile impulses. Drake reprints a photograph of Sara at age five, looking cute for the photographer, but clenching her right fist by her side, perhaps to help her suppress her inner feelings.

Sara was taught at home until she was nine. Thereafter, she attended private schools. Her parents discouraged her from playing with other children because of her frailty, and she became rather shy. At school, Sara did not go to parties, engage in athletics or have typical teenage fun. She was asked to be on the commencement program, but she declined the honor.

Although her parents were not especially interested in literature, Sara soon developed a passion for it, and her older brothers and sisters encouraged her poetic gift. The schools she attended gave her an excellent education in literature and the arts so that, even without a college education, Sara was well-read and informed.

The Young Adult

At school, Sara made several close friends and, after graduation, this group formed the nucleus of a group of women interested in the arts. They called themselves the Potters, and they decided to produce an artistic monthly magazine containing their literary and artistic efforts. Each month they produced just a single copy of The Potter's Wheel, from November 1904 until October 1907, thirty-six issues in all. The group also wanted to improve their skills, and so criticism was encouraged. Sara's poems first appeared in print in this magazine, and her first published book of poems contained many of these poems. From the beginning, Sara was very conscientious about her writing and distressed by flaws in her poems. She worked hard to improve them and relied on her associates for constructive criticism.

In this phase of her life, Sara was involved with a group of women, and friendship with women continued to play a major role for the rest of her life. In the Potters, Williamina Parrish played a prominent role in Sara's life, helping her organize the poems for her first collection. The women in these years played a nurturing and guiding role, taking the place of her mother in supporting her, and Sara always seemed to need someone to help her complete a book of poems. (After Williamina Parrish, there was Marion Stanley, Jessie Rittenhouse, Marguerite Wilkinson, and finally Margaret Conklin) Later, however, she became less dependent upon them, and her final friend (Margaret Conklin) was more like a servant/daughter to Sara. In Sara's early years her heroes were women - Sappho, Guenevere and the modern Eleonora Duse. Nonetheless, she also needed fantasy male figures for her love poems. Until she was twenty-eight, though, the lovers about whom she wrote poems were almost entirely imaginary.

In 1905, Sara and her mother took a trip abroad for three months. By the time the boat reached Greece, which for a long time had fascinated Sara, she was ill with a fever. But she managed a little sightseeing and recovered enough to visit the Holy Lands, Egypt, Italy, Paris and London. Sara enjoyed the trip immensely and took many trips abroad during the rest of her life.

The fame of The Potter's Wheel spread through the literary circles of St Louis, eventually reaching the attention of William Reedy who ran the St Louis Mirror. He included a piece by Sara for the first time in May 1906, and her pieces in the Mirror soon began to establish her reputation as a lyric poet.

In 1907, Poet Lore accepted one of her sonnets and later that year produced a book of poems for her which her family had to subsidize. Reviews of the book, in The Saturday Review of London for example, were favorable. In 1908, she had a poem accepted in Atlantic Monthly, and Putnams brought out a book of her poems in 1911. Reviews in The New York Times and Current Literature praised it, and she became a member of the recently founded Poetry Society Of America. From the first, Sara had the tenacity to submit her work again and again to periodicals until it was accepted. She shrewdly sent copies of her books to supportive reviewers, and she cultivated friends in the literary field.

Sara continued to live at home, in a suite of rooms on the second floor, with a door isolating her from the rest of the house. Friends did not drop in on her casually. Rather, close friends had fixed, scheduled meetings, and their visits were kept brief so as not to overtax Sara's health. There were two main sides to Sara: this distraught, sickly person who withdrew into isolation, and a witty, intelligent and candid companion. However, this social side appeared only with those whom she knew well, and Sara preferred to develop new relationships through exchanges of letters.

There is no evidence that Sara was especially sickly. She had illnesses and fevers to be sure, but perhaps no more than the average person. Sara would get involved in social activities, and these seemed to arouse desires in her that she could not cope with. At this point, she would retreat into exhaustion and sickness and withdraw to a clinic or a hotel away from everyone to reorganize herself. Sara herself once wondered whether, had she been born into a poor family, she would have had better health! More likely, if she had not been so suppressed as a child and so repressed as an adult, she would have no need for retreating into sickness.

In both 1908 and 1909, Sara's health continued to be poor [7], and so she spent some time in San Antonio and at a hospital in Connecticut hoping to recover. Thereafter, when life became too much for her to handle, she escaped to this hospital under the guise of being sick. In San Antonio, she made the acquaintance of another poet, Marion Stanley, with whom she developed a close friendship. Marion tried to get Sara to see herself honestly and to get out of the path of sickliness she had entered. However, even though every visit back home to her parents and St Louis brought on depression (and a desire for death) and a retreat into the patient role, Sara did not appear to have the strength to leave home and try to build a healthy life for herself. Sara was overwhelmed by the aggressive vitality of her mother, and the patient role was how she and her mother had learned to relate to each other in a semblance of a loving relationship.

In 1909, though, Sara decided that she did not want to live at home with her parents for ever, especially with her domineering and suffocating mother, but neither did she want to be independent and support herself. (If she ever had to do that, she said, she would kill herself.) She decided that she needed a husband to support her. So she began to look around.

In 1908, Sara had begun a correspondence with a poet in New York City, John O'Hara, which developed into a life-long friendship. However, Sara developed an infatuation with O'Hara which was fueled by her fantasies about him made possible by the fact that she had never met him face-to-face. Indeed, she was scared by the prospect of real love and avoided meeting O'Hara on several occasions. She eventually met him in the January of 1911, and this meeting introduced reality into her relationship with him.

In 1911, Sara persuaded her parents to let her go to New York (at twenty-seven, she still needed their permission), and she began visiting New York for meetings of the Poetry Society, building up close relationships with writers there. When away from New York, she kept in touch with friends there by letter. Interestingly, when she was in New York, Sara showed little of the exhaustion and illness that plagued her in St Louis.

In the summer of 1912, Sara and Jessie Rittenhouse took a trip to Europe, and on the boat back Sara met Stafford Hatfield, an Englishman, with whom she became infatuated. It is not clear whether he wanted Sara to become his lover or return to England with him. But

---

[7] Sara's illnesses during her life consisted mainly of colds, sore throats, influenza, stomach pains, bladder inflammations, fever blisters, indigestion, flatulence, facial neuralgia, headaches, bronchitis, and back and neck pains.

Sara could not cope with her anxiety, and she fled back to St Louis. From afar, Hatfield no longer was as interested in Sara as he had once seemed, and eventually he ended the relationship. This episode persuaded Sara that she had to plan more purposefully to get married or else she would remain a spinster. Since erotic emotions scared her, perhaps rationality could find her a husband?

The next romantic figure was John Wheelock, also a poet. But though Sara fell in love with him and gave him every opportunity to declare his love for her, he never did. In 1913, Sara began a correspondence Vachel Lindsay, also a poet, and they finally met in 1914 in St. Louis. After this meeting, they wrote to each other more often, and eventually Vachel fell in love with her. However, in 1914 Sara was introduced to Ernst Filsinger, who was running a shoe business in St Louis. He too was attracted to Sara, and soon Sara had to choose which one to marry. John Wheeler was still the man she loved, she thought, but he did not want her. So she had to choose from two men, neither of whom she loved, but who seemed to love her.

In 1914, Sara's father had suffered a stoke and her mother's health was also poor. These events happened at a critical point for Sara. The poor health of her parents made the question of what would happen to her once they died more urgent. Vachel was poor, too full of energy and too egocentric to be a caring husband for Sara. Ernst appeared to fit the role much better. Their interests and natures seemed harmonious, and he appeared to worship her. He would make a good husband and father for her children. Despite Sara's misgivings, which she did not tell anyone till many years later, they married in December 1914 in St Louis.

The marriage was a disaster from the beginning. Sara could not abide sleeping with a man, and so they always had separate bedrooms, at home, in hotels, and even on board boats. Sex too, apparently, was a disaster. Sara developed a bladder problem that caused excruciating pain soon after the wedding which lasted for two years. That probably limited their sexual relationship. (Sara would probably have had difficulty having a sexual relationship even with a man she loved passionately given the way she was raised.) More importantly, Sara never could feel passionately in love with Ernst.

Life must have been difficult for Sara at this point. She had chosen the conventional life of marriage partly to get away from her parents, partly for security, and partly because it she was a conventional person who expected to live conventionally. But since love was missing, and passion too, she had failed. She was faced with a difficult interpersonal relationship, an absence of love, but probable future unhappiness. [8] Sara had one solution open to her. She retreated into illness again.

---

[8] Sara did respect Ernst and was grateful to him for the love he felt for her and for the care and respect with which he always treated her.

They made their home first in St Louis and then in New York City, and they chose to live in hotel apartments to spare Sara the strain of running a house and staff. Ernst was proud of Sara's poetic talent and encouraged her in every way he could. Her third book of poems appeared in 1915 from Macmillan, again receiving excellent reviews. And her next book of poems in 1918 received a prize that was the forerunner of the Pulitzer Prize.

Married life soon developed a clear pattern. Sara continued to write poems and edit collections. Ernst became involved in international trade and was called upon to travel the world widely, but at a pace that would strain Sara too much. So she stayed in New York and took trips to secluded spots around America. Sara continued to be frail, so that even socializing was restricted. She would send Ernst in her place occasionally to read her poems and to important meetings, and even to social events with her friends for company. Ernst screened her mail when she was away and occasionally handled her business affairs. Sara even turned down honors because they would involve evening dinners or travel.

Very soon a conflict developed in their relationship. Ernst's new job, after his shoe business went bankrupt, was in international trade. He became an expert on the topic. He gave talks all over America and travelled all over the world. Sara encouraged him in this, since she wanted him to be successful and she also wanted financial security. But she also resented the fact that he threw himself so energetically into his work. She was continually telling him to take it easy. (Ernst probably threw himself into his work because of the frustrations arising out of his marriage!)

Then again, she missed him a lot at first when he began to travel though, after he came back, she seemed unable to cope with him in their apartment. She would become depressed, fall ill and take herself off to her hospital in Connecticut or to a favorite vacation spot. In fact she seemed most content off by herself in hospital or resort hotel as long as Ernst stayed in New York City.

However, much as she found life with Ernst difficult, at least his presence kept her depression at bay and took her mind off self-destructive thoughts. Ernst's absences brought Sara closest to feelings of love for him.

Surprisingly, in 1917 Sara became pregnant. Although she had thought she wanted to be a mother, the reality of it now threatened to interfere with her career. More importantly, it threatened her role as patient. How could Sara cope with taking care of someone else? So she had an abortion. Of course, she could justify an abortion on the grounds of her frail health, but she must also have felt a great deal of guilt over her decision.

For much of their life, their financial position was not secure. Though they could afford a comfortable life style, especially supplemented by Sara's earnings from her writings, in early years they had to borrow from Ernst's family to get by. Sara considered ways of increasing her contribution to their income, but she never did much about it.

The absences caused by Ernst's traveling grew. In 1920 and 1921, they were together just six weeks in a period of a year and a half. Sarcasm grew more common between them, they brought up old annoyances, and they readily got hurt over new trifles. Ernst grew more defensive, moody and irritable, and his explosive temper showed itself more.

The Divorce and Final Years

Sara's decision to divorce Ernst in 1929 came as a surprise to her friends. Sara feared abandonment, and this fear had been made worse by his absences. (In a letter Sara wrote to Ernst just before he sailed on the trip during which she would divorce him, she listed his previous trips in 1919, 1919-1920, 1923, 1925, 1928, and now the present one.) Eventually she began to fear that he would be attracted to another woman. (This was likely, of course, since she would not be his lover and since he was away a lot. However, there is no evidence that Ernst ever behaved in any way as to reinforce these fears.)

She had discussed divorce with Ernst before, but he had protested. So she planned the divorce in Nevada while he was away. She divorced him for mental cruelty and begged him not to contest it. Although she expressed euphoria at being free when she was back in New York, she soon sank into a depression. After the divorce, Sara lived in hotel apartments by herself, just as her marriage had consisted of living in hotel apartments mainly by herself while Ernst was away. Her life changed little, except that Ernst no longer made occasional visits!

Sara met a young student, Margaret Conklin, who became her close friend in her final years. Margaret would visit daily, and they went to Europe together. However, interestingly, Sara showed little concern for Margaret. She ate meals sent up to her from the hotel in front of Margaret without ever worrying whether Margaret had eaten. Sara had been in the patient role all of her life, with others taking care of her, so that she had never learned that sometimes one has to take care of others. If Margaret upset Sara in some trivial way, she would even be banished for days at a time.

Sara grew more inflexible. She still gave friends specific appointment times for their visits, and now she kept them waiting if they arrived a few minutes early. These latter years illustrated quite clearly her egocentricity, her lack of caring for others, and her selfishness.

In the final years of her marriage, Sara had experienced periods during which she could not write. She went from the summer of 1920 till November without writing one poem. These long barren spells became quite common. Five months in 1925. More during the period leading up to her divorce. But even after the divorce, writing was not easy.

Sara had experienced depressions throughout her life. In later years she lost weight. She suffered from insomnia, though in her creative periods she would work on her poems during the night, and she also had trouble getting up in the mornings, typical symptoms of depression. She took Veronal as a sleeping tablet. Her moods varied with the seasons. Her depressions were worse in winter, and she hated the cold weather since it brought on her respiratory illnesses. As she grew older, external events led to an intensification of her depression (such as the marital problems of her friends, the Untermeyers, and the suicide of their son).

Sara's father died in 1921 at the age of eighty-two, and this was a severe loss for Sara. Her mother died in 1924, as did her older brother George. In 1928, a friend, Marguerite Wilkinson, drowned after recovering from a nervous breakdown. Later that year, Sara was injured in taxicab accident. In September of the year, Ernst's father died.

Sara's concerns over her finances grew. After her parents' death, the inheritance was not as great as had been expected. The stock market crash in 1929 also increased her anxiety. After the divorce, though she had asked for no alimony, Sara tried to get Ernst to set up a trust fund for her. She worried whether she could afford to renew the lease in her hotel and decided to move a cheaper apartment. Her concerns became almost a nightmarish obsession. However, she left almost eighty-four thousand dollars, and so it appears that her financial concerns were irrational.

After her divorce in 1929, many of Sara's friends moved away from New York City, and she was often lonely. Despite craving company, she often rejected offers from friends to visit her, pleading illness. In 1931 Vachel Lindsay killed himself by drinking Lysol, and Sara was distraught over this. For many months after Lindsay's suicide, Sara feared that she was about to have a complete physical breakdown or die in an accident.

Sara was no longer able to write productively, but John Wheelock suggested she write a biography of Christina Rossetti. Macmillan gave her advance on the project, and she had written about a hundred pages at the time of her death.

In August 1932, Sara went to England to gather material for the biography but got pneumonia. She came back to America in September, 1932, still sick, and recovery was slow. She was very weak and deeply depressed. She had failed to build a fruitful life after the divorce, and now only ill health seem to lay ahead for her. She worried that her heart had weakened and that her blood pressure was fluctuating too much. Her friends were very concerned over her despondency. She was taking sleeping pills regularly and seemed severely depressed.

During the Fall, the deaths of some friends deepened her despondency, and in December she began to accumulate a supply of sleeping pills. She began to fear having a stoke, like her father and her brother John (who had lived for twenty years after a paralytic stroke, dying in 1917 at the age of forty-seven).

In December, she went to Florida to stay with Jessie Rittenhouse but lay in bed all day with the drapes closed. Jessie discussed the situation with Sara's doctor and nurse and they all felt she should return to New York and seek psychiatric help. She developed an obsessive but unfounded fear that her blood vessels were beginning to rupture, increasing her fear of a stroke. On January 27, 1933, a blood vessel did break in her hand, making her frantic with the idea that her long-awaited stroke was imminent.

On the evening of January 29, 1933, Margaret Conklin visited her. They read and listened to Beethoven's Fifth Symphony. Sara was found the next morning at 9 am by her nurse, dead in her bath after taking an overdose of sedatives. The water was still warm, and perhaps the nurse could have saved her had she checked earlier.

Discussion

Drake (1979) points out that four major women poets of the Nineteenth Century (Emily Bronte, Christina Rossetti, Emily Dickinson and Elizabeth Barrett Browning until she was forty) were all recluses like Sara. All four belonged to very close family units which fulfilled their desires for affection and intellectual stimulation. Sara ventured out more than some of her predecessors but continually retreated into seclusion because of her "illnesses", becoming almost a total recluse by the end of her life.

The Victorian era encouraged women in the creative arts but undermined their self-confidence. They were allowed to dabble, but they were not supposed to achieve. When they did write poetry, they wrote mostly about love, protective love and the desire to submit to the ideal lover. However, it was not always easy to find this in their own lives. They often ended up renouncing love for men and substituting an attraction to death. They frequently had mysterious physical weaknesses and chronic ill health, a neurotic way of resolving the conflict between their personal desires and the conventions imposed upon them by the society.

Sara was a chronically depressed woman whose depression worsened as she grew older. In her middle age, concerns that were mild as a young adult grew to be irrational obsessions. She feared poverty and an imminent death, though neither was very likely. It is unfortunate that Sara would contract a real illness (pneumonia) at this time and that a blood vessel did break in her hand. Her irrational concerns no longer seemed so irrational to her.

She had struggled to lead a conventional life but failed. Sara never learned to form and maintain healthy interpersonal relationships. The patient role she learned as a child was of no use to her in marriage. Simply put, she failed to mature. She remained a child, as evidenced by her failed marriage and the self-centeredness she displayed in her friendships.

Her childhood experiences led her to repress her basic emotions. Anger, curiosity of the world, sexuality were all suppressed by her aged parents, and in particular by her mother. She married at thirty with no realistic idea of the responsibilities of a person involved in adult relationships.

The prospect of having a child frightened her so much that she had an abortion. In looking for an event that could have turned her life around, this might have been it. The easiest change for a person to make in life is to switch to a role that is complementary to one that she has already had. Perhaps Sara could have become the nurse (mother) taking care of the patient (her baby) after her years of experience as the patient? But maybe not. Anyway, Sara panicked and avoided the experience.

By the end of her life, she was finding it hard to write creatively, she was lonely and isolated, and her irrational fears and depressions were getting worse. Sara had often contemplated death, and now she planned it. She had long used sleeping pills and knew the peace they brought her. And so she sought the ultimate peace, not in bed, but in a warm bath, as if seeking the womb from which she may have wished that she had never emerged.

References

Bosworth, P. Diane Arbus. New York: Knopf, 1984. Butscher, E. Sylvia Plath. New York: Seabury, 1976.
Clarke, R. V., & Lester D. Suicide: closing the exits. New York: Springer-Verlag, 1989.
Drake, W. Sara Teasdale. New York: Harper & Row, 1979.
Laing, R. D. The divided self. New York: Pantheon, 1960.
Lester, D., & Terry, R. The use of poetry therapy: lessons from the life of Anne Sexton. The Arts in Psychotherapy, 1992, 19, 47-52.
Middlebrook, D. W. Anne Sexton. Boston: Houghton-Mifflin, 1991.

Chapter 5

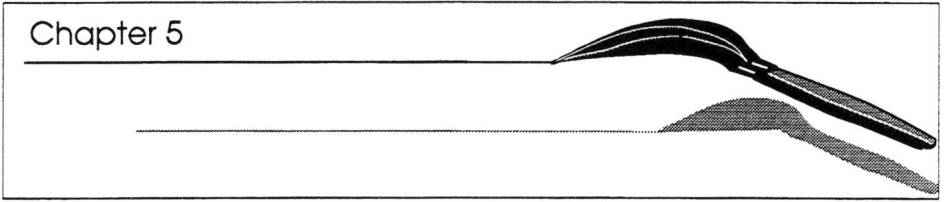

FOUR NONSUICIDAL CREATIVE WOMEN

In Chapter 4, we presented the lives of the four remaining creative women who committed suicide. In this chapter we will present the lives of the four remaining creative women who died of natural causes.

Colette[1]

Colette's parents lived in Saint-Sauveur, about 120 miles south of Paris, France, a part of Burgundy. Her mother, Adele Sidonie Landoy, known as Sido, was born in Paris in 1835. Sido's mother died soon thereafter, and Sido was raised by her brothers in Belgium. At the age of twenty-one she took her first husband, a landowner in Saint-Sauveur, Jules Robineau-Duclos, twice her age. Although he had inherited property and added to it, he was a brutal drunkard. She had two children by him, Juliette and Achille, before he died eight years later. In 1865, she quickly remarried a local man, Jules Colette, with whom she might have been having an affair before her first husband's death. Born in 1829, Jules Colette had served in the military, lost a leg while fighting for Napoleon III in Italy, and retired to Saint-Sauveur. Colette always kept his military record, a photograph of him in uniform and his medals with her. He had ambition but achieved nothing. He lost elections, saw himself as a writer but never wrote, and was a terrible businessman, eventually losing all of the property his wife had inherited after her first husband's death.

---

[1] This section is based on Lottman (1991).

Their first child was Leopold, and Sidonie Gabrielle Colette, later known simply as Colette, was born on January 28, 1873. Colette's mother was an avid reader and introduced Colette to literature at an early age. Colette was only seven when she discovered the works of Balzac and became infatuated with them. One scholar has found references to fifty-five characters from Balzac in Colette's novels.

Colette began at the humble village school just before her sixth birthday in 1878, and she passed her first diploma at the age of twelve. The village then created a secondary program and hired a headmistress. Colette was intelligent and gifted, particularly in French and music, but also a trouble maker. Luckily her teacher liked her cheekiness. Colette passed her final exams in 1889.

At that point, the Colettes had to sell their house, and they moved to live, first, with Sido's son Achille, and then in a house opposite him in a nearby town where he was a doctor. School was over for Colette, but she had found a husband.

Henri Gauthier-Villars, known as Willy, was a Parisian journalist (born in 1859). He had come to Saint-Sauveur because a family there was raising an illegitimate son of his whom the mother had abandoned. His father was an old comrade-at-arms of Jules Colette. He met Colette when she was ten, and she was in love him by the time she was sixteen. They may have become lovers when Colette was nineteen during a visit to Paris. Though her parents opposed the marriage, his family urged it. After a three-year engagement, they were married on May 15, 1893, when she was twenty.

Colette's Apprenticeship

Willy was beginning to build a writing career. He had set up a process in which others wrote for him. They wrote novels, reviews of books and the theater, and other pieces to which he signed his name. His helpers included people destined for fame, such as Claude Debussy. He was an authority on most things and invited to a multitude of social and literary salons, theaters and cafes. His literary factory produced fifty books before it broke down. Colette later said that his own talent often exceeded those who wrote for him, and that sometimes it would have been simpler if he had written the piece to which he signed his name.

Soon after their marriage, she found him with a mistress, with whom she later became good friends, a practice which she continued with the lovers of her other husbands. But to compensate for the trials of the new bride, there was the social life. She became friends with Anatole France, Marcel Proust, Gabriel Faure, and many other leading writers, musicians, and intellectuals of the era.

Colette's name was attached to some reviews first in 1895, and she wrote her first review in 1896. Willy encouraged her to write about her early life to see if he could use the material. Although initially he rejected her writing, he later saw its merit and the result was <u>Claudine At School</u> published under Willy's name which appeared in book form in 1900.

To write the sequels, they bought a country house where Colette could write, and each year saw a new Claudine book, <u>Claudine in Paris</u>, <u>Claudine Married</u>, and <u>Claudine and Annie</u>. The original manuscript of the third book survives, and it is in Colette's handwriting, though the changes introduced by Willy are also clear. Colette's first book under her own name (though she signed it "Colette Willy") appeared in 1904, a collection of playlets involving animals (<u>Dialogues de Betes</u>). Another book (<u>Minne</u>) appeared that year which she had written, but Willy's name appeared on it. Later Colette republished it with its sequel as <u>The Innocent Libertine</u> (in 1909).

Meanwhile stress had entered into the marriage. Willy continued to have lovers, and Colette too. Indeed there is a tale of them having the same (female) lover at one point. In May 1905, they agreed to a separation of their property. Willy took up with a mistress, Meg (Marguerite Maniez), while Colette had a female lover, Missy (Mathilde de Morny, the Marquise de Belbeuf), forty two years old. Strangely though, Colette and Willy continued to travel together, often with their lovers, and Colette and Meg became good friends. Colette's father died in September that year, just short of his seventy-sixth birthday, and Willy and Colette drove down for the funeral.

Independence

Colette decided to take up a career on the stage. She worked initially with Georges Wague in pantomine, and her first performance was in <u>Love, Desire and the Chimera</u>, in February 1906. She was good enough, or at least enough people were willing to pay to see this famous writer and subject of scandal, that she continued to work in the theater for many years. There were, however, many critics of her acting over the years, none of whom managed to dampen her enthusiasm or that of her audiences. Eventually Missy appeared with Colette on the stage. Many of Colette's books are based on her experiences, and characters from her past and present life appear in them. This blending of reality and fiction held great interest for readers (and theatergoers). In 1908, at the age of thirty-five, she played Claudine in the stage adaptions of the novels, thereby playing a character based on what audiences knew to be her own life.

Colette also continued to write, working on the last of the Claudine books by herself, Retreat from Love. She moved to an apartment just around the corner from Missy's, but the four lovers (Colette and Missy, Willy and Meg) spent much time together, and perhaps Colette and Meg were lovers too.

Willy finally sued for divorce, on the grounds of desertion, and a legal separation was granted in February 1907. (The divorce became final in June, 1910.) Colette could now sign her books as Colette Willy (she eventually switched to just Colette). There were signs, however, that both regretted the break. When Colette and Missy found a vacation house on the Channel coast, near Dieppe, Willy and Meg came as neighbors. Yet frictions over the writing business still arose, especially after Willy sold the rights to the first four Claudine books for a lump sum for himself and sold their house near Besancon. By 1910, Colette and Willy were no longer on speaking terms. He died in 1931, alone and in debt.

Colette generated a steady stream of income from her essays and novels, all of which appeared first in newspapers and magazines before being published as books, from her acting, and from a variety of other activities, including editing a series of books, writing and posing for commercial advertisements, writing subtitles for American films, writing newspaper articles, adapting her books for the stage and eventually for film, lecturing, writing plays and screen plays, a weekly radio program, and in the 1930s developing a line of beauty products and opening beauty shops. And during all of this, which involved hectic touring and balancing the demands of her various activities, Colette also carefully observed her surroundings and wrote about them for newspapers.

Despite this continual flow of income, Colette was always urgently in need of money, and so she wrote or performed simply to ensure income to provide for the next few weeks. More ambitious work often had to be laid aside at those times.

For a while, Missy took care of Colette as lover, companion and friend. They dined out regularly, vacationed together and sometimes went on Colette's tours together. Eventually they bought a house on the Brittany coast, near Saint-Malo. But Colette continued to be a free spirit. In 1910, she went off to Capri with a lover, Auguste Heriot, and in 1911 for a holiday with a female friend, Lily de Reme, but Missy seems not to have been too disturbed.

Then she met Henry de Jouvenel, born in 1876, a titled country gentleman, who had earned a degree in philosophy from the Sorbonne and become a writer. He married the daughter of the owner of the newspaper Le Matin, had a son Bertrand, and divorced. He had a lover, Isabelle de Comminges, by whom he also had a son, Renaud. By the time he met Colette, he was one of the two editors-in-chief of Le Matin. By 1911 they were lovers.

His former lover, Isabelle, was upset and threatened to kill Colette, but ran off with Colette's former lover, Auguste Heriot, instead. Soon Colette was settled in the Jouvenel home, Castel-Novel in the Correze, and his house in Paris. Despite a major row in the summer of 1912, Colette got pregnant, and they were married in December 1912. (Colette's mother died that September.) Her daughter, Colette de Jouvenal des Ursins, was born on July 3, 1913. Since both parents had careers which involved a great deal of travel, the younger Colette was raised by a nurse until she was eight and ready for boarding school.

The war sent Colette to Paris while Henry was called up. Although he was a reservist, he was soon at the front, initially at Verdun. Colette visited him there, and even lived in secret with him there for a time, all the while writing pieces for the newspapers on the war. (Her daughter was with an English nurse down at Castel-Novel.) Henry was eventually sent to Italy to work at the allied conferences, and Colette now wrote dispatches from Italy. The end of the war saw Henry back in charge at Le Matin with Colette as the drama critic. Pauline, a teenage housemaid from Correze came to help in the house and remained Colette's helper until Colette's death.

After the war, Colette began to befriend Henry's son by his first wife, Bertrand (born in 1903). He visited them a lot and stayed with them for long periods, so much so that his mother worried about him being corrupted. To no avail. Colette and Bertrand became lovers. (Of course, Henry too had taken many lovers.) In the 1920s, Colette and Henry drifted apart, spending less and less time with each other. In 1923, Henry fell in love with Marthe Bibesco, a Rumanian aristocrat who wrote fiction, and perhaps he was upset over Colette's involvement with his son. He let Colette sue for divorce (which became final in 1925), but this left Colette almost broke again. (Henry died in 1935.)

Almost immediately, she met Maurice Goudeket, born in 1889, a writer who now made his living selling pearls, sixteen years younger than Colette (who was fifty-two) and never married. They married in April, 1935. Their relationship lasted until her death. She sold the house in Brittany and bought one at Saint-Tropez for them on the Riviera.

Colette's written work became better and better. Mitsou written in 1917 was her first work of fiction not based on her own life. Proust thought her writing good, as did Francois Mauriac and Andrè Gide. Leading critics praised it. After Cheri was published in 1920, Colette was awarded membership in the Legion of Honor and gradually rose in the Order (Officer in 1928, Commander in 1936, and the cross in 1953, the highest rank that any woman had ever attained). In 1936 she was elected to Belgian Royal Academy of French Language and Literature. Cheri was made into a play, and for the one hundredth performance Colette took the lead role. The first serious study of her writing appeared in 1927. Now when she traveled to lecture, she was treated with great honor, received by Ambassadors, Presidents, and Kings.

In the 1930s, illnesses began to plague her. In 1931, she tripped and broke her leg. In 1934, she developed neuritis in her writing arm. In 1937, a tenant in the Palais-Royal apartments in Paris, where she had lived for a while, heard that she wanted to move back there, and he let her take over his apartment, one she had long desired. She and Maurice moved in, and they stayed there for the rest of her life. They sold their house in Saint-Tropez and bought one near Montfort-l'Amaury.

At the beginning of the Second World War, Colette and Maurice first continued to live in Paris, but then fled, first to Montfort-l'Amaury, then to a house in Vichy France owned by the de Jouvenels but left to Colette. Eventually they decided to return to Paris and, after being turned back at the border once, managed to get into German-occupied France and to Paris.

Maurice was Jewish (and Hitler's ambassador to France knew this), and they lived in fear of him being arrested and deported. Colette's connections prevented this until December 12, 1941. Colette made great efforts to get him released (using her friendship with the wife of the German ambassador), and he was released on February 6, 1942. In May, he and Colette had tea at the Ambassador's residence! After the release, Maurice stayed close to home and slept at nights in the attic of the building. He fled to Saint-Tropez for a while, but then returned to Paris.

The wartime was difficult, but Colette's friends sent her food parcels from Vichy France. She wrote for the German-controlled press and publishing houses, but she managed to avoid providing any political support for the Nazis, and so she was not censured after the war, unlike other writers who were executed or sent to prison. Her arthritis and rheumatism grew worse, and she tried all manner of treatments for the pain (x-rays, intravenous injections of sulfur and iodine, and acupuncture), all of which proved ineffective.

She celebrated her seventy-second birthday in January, 1945, in liberated Paris. She now could rarely leave her apartment, and so a steady stream of visitors arrived there to meet and talk with her. In May, 1945, she was elected to the prestigious Goncourt Academy (and became the President of the Academy in 1949) which awarded an annual literary prize. The meetings of the jurors often had to be at her apartment since she could not easily leave it.

Finances were a little more secure. Maurice had formed a company to publish Colette's works, and the company purchased the apartment in which they lived. In 1950, they traveled annually to Monte Carlo where they were entertained royally. But Colette's health continued to worsen, and she died in on August 3, 1954, at the age of eighty-one.

Discussion

Colette's life is remarkable for the fact that her biographer gives few clues as to how this rural teenager developed both into a great writer and a sexually and socially liberated woman. Her childhood seems relatively free from trauma except for the financial problems of her parents. Relatively uneducated, she appears to have learned to write under the guidance of her first husband, Willy. He too seems to have introduced her into the intellectual social world and to its liberated sexuality, a milieu in which she felt at ease. She took up acting, again without formal training, and built a successful career on the stage. And despite her stage career, she was finally accepted into the literary academies of honor.

She was lucky in her three husbands, each of whom provided important resources for her in the different stages of her life. And she certainly seems to have been free of any psychiatric disorder. She had a full life and a busy life. Though it was filled with stress, Colette coped well with the crises she faced.

Amy Lowell[2]

The Lowells arrived in America in 1639, twenty years after the *Mayflower*. They rose to become one of the leading New England families, if not the leading family. (It was the Cabots who spoke only to the Lowells, and the Lowells who spoke only to God!) Amy's father, Augustus Lowell, was born in 1830, graduated from Harvard, and married Katherine Lawrence, the daughter of his father's business partner, in 1854.

Percival was born in 1855, Lawrence in 1956, then twins of whom only Katherine survived, and Elizabeth (Bessie). Mrs Lowell then developed Bright's disease. After visiting spas to Europe to help her recovery, the Lowells bought an estate in Brookline (Massachusetts) which they called Sevenels and kept a house in Boston for the winter.

---

[2] This section is based on Gould (1975).

After another daughter died soon after birth, Mrs. Lowell gave birth to her final child, Amy, on February 9, 1874. Amy's mother remained a semi-invalid for all of Amy's life, and Amy was raised mainly by her nurse-governness. Her father had little time for Amy at first but, as she grew older, let her help him in his gardens, a hobby which Amy adopted.

Early on, she showed initiative. She persuaded the coachman to teach her to drive the horses, though she never liked riding them, and she was difficult to order around. (In fact, she was more likely to obey the coachman than her parents.) She did not have the companionship of other children and was often lonely, and so she took up the interests which her father and older brothers had. She grew especially close to Percy, and friends thought that she would much rather have been a boy. She preferred outdoor games and activities and was a regular tomboy by age eight.

Stimulated by the distinguished adults she lived with and who visited the Lowells, she was precocious. She became a good conversationalist, amusing her parents' guests with puns. One of her witty lines was published in Life, a precursor of the Harvard Lampoon. She loved to perform in front of guests. She liked approval but was self-confident enough to tolerate failure.

She became plump quite early in life and showed a disinclination to get up early, traits which became increasingly strong. A trip to Europe with her parents in 1882 was enjoyable, but the stress of travel, together with a visit to see instruments of torture at Nuremburg made her ill and fearful for several months afterwards. Although her spelling was poor, she liked to write, and her parents encouraged her to keep a journal on their trip across America in 1883. She wrote her first poem in this journal. At ten she started a mimeographed magazine called "The Monthly Story-Teller," and her mother encouraged her to put together a book for sale at a charity bazaar. Amy called it Dream Drops.

She was sent to a variety of private schools, where she made friends with the students and enemies of the teachers. Though knowledgeable, she was a smart-aleck and not interested in getting good grades. However, she loved to read.

As a teenager, she continued to be plump. Her physique caused her despair, humiliation and self-hatred, and she lacked a close female friend during these years. She fell in love with an occasional boy, but she kept these infatuations to herself. The dancing classes for those about to become debutants were her worst trial.

She thought of going to Radcliffe, but the teaching she had at her school and the lectures she attended at Radcliffe so bored her that she declined to go to college and quit school at the age of seventeen. She educated herself by reading, both at home and at the Boston Athenaeum. She discovered the poems of Keats and a book by Leigh Hunt

(Imagination and Fancy) which thrilled her. Hunt wrote in the style Amy thought teachers should have. Reading Keats changed her self-image, and she became a little more self-confident. She practiced dancing with friends and she became a good and sought-after dance partner when she came out in 1891.

Amy's mother grew quite ill, was often in severe pain, complained that nobody loved her and was sometimes deranged. Amy was the only one who was around to attend to her, and she feared that she too might lose her mind like her mother. Her mother died in April, 1895, when Amy was twenty-one.

Percy meanwhile had traveled to the Orient and written four books on the Orient and on astronomy. Lawrence had also published books (on government). Amy decided that she too would pursue a literary career, and she experimented for several years with plays, novels and short stories.

In 1897, Amy may have received a proposal of marriage from a young man who then broke it off. She was terribly upset and spent days alone in her room. She then became determined to diet and to do this she followed a popular method which involved traveling abroad and restricting food intake. She went to Egypt with friends and returned with the same weight but also with gastritis which produced a nervous prostration which lasted for seven years. She suffered from terrible headaches and abdominal bloating during this time, and she decided thereafter to accept her plumpness.

After a trip to England in 1899, she returned to find her father ill, and he died that summer. Amy bought the Brookline estate from her siblings and began to remodel it to suit herself. She created a large library in which she could also put on plays. She also created a music room for concerts. She had the house electrified, and she bought a summer home in New Hampshire. She joined various civic boards and shocked the local gentry by speaking up in meetings (unusual for women in those days).

In 1902, when she was twenty-eight, she saw the European actress, Eleanor Duse, perform in Boston. Amy was so moved that she came home and wrote a poem, met the actress and followed the troupe on its tour around America. She decided at that time to become a poet, and she worked hard at it, putting aside the headaches, the attacks of nerves and her depressions.

The Poet

Amy submitted four poems to Atlantic Monthly which were accepted. The first appeared in August 1910. She organized her first book of poems and persuaded Houghton-Mifflin to publish it. A Dome of Many-Colored Glass came out in October 1912 to tepid reviews. The poems were not exciting enough. Her disappointment brought on her gastritis, and she spent some time in bed.

But undaunted she continued and, after having some poems accepted by Poetry, Amy saw in that magazine an article by Ezra Pound on a group of poets to which he belonged called the Imagists. Amy was impressed by the group's work and realized that she too wanted to write in that style. She travelled to London to meet the poets in the group.

At the same time, Amy began to be noticed. She had taken up smoking cigars, and this made headlines in the New York Tribune. Amy saw that this kind of publicity would help her establish a public image and contribute to the success of her poetry. So she cultivated the image, even though it was natural for her to behave in the way she did. She smoked, she bullied, she stayed in bed till past noon, and she received visitors in her bedroom while still in bed.

Amy was helped in her endeavors by the many strong friendships she developed. One of the first was with Carl Engel, a composer and music publisher. With his encouragement, she put on and acted in plays at Sevenels and organized monthly concerts. Then, in 1912, Amy met an actress who was visiting Boston, Ada Dwyer, and they became close friends. Ada, born in Salt Lake City in 1863, had been married, given birth to a daughter, and divorced. Within two years of meeting Amy, Ada had quit the stage and moved in with Amy, and they became devoted companions for the remainder of Amy's life. Amy tried to be possessive and restrictive, not wanting Ada to leave her for a moment, but she soon realized that she would lose Ada if she gave her no freedom. So Ada went off occasionally to visit her relatives in Salt Lake City and her daughter.

Amy also worked hard at selling her work and that of other poets she admired. She read her poetry whenever she was asked, and she soon began to be in demand as a lecturer on both poetry and music. Her lectures were well prepared and usually published, first as magazine articles and then as books. She visited editors of magazines and her publishers (first Houghton-Mifflin and then Macmillan) selling them on her poems and ideas for books. She edited several volumes of poets who could be considered Imagists and a volume on six French poets. At her salons she introduced her audiences to new music, including Bartok, Debussy and Satie.

At the outbreak of the First World War, Amy and Ada were in England. There, Amy developed a friendship with D. H. Lawrence and thereafter always supported his writing in whatever way she could. She worked for the Belgian War Relief in London under Herbert Hoover and helped stranded Americans return home. Amy and Ada returned to America in September 1914.

Her second volume of poems appeared that month, <u>Sword Blades and Poppy Seeds</u>, and this time she made a splash. Her poems had varied rhythms and versification, and the reviews came in angry, favorable or puzzled. No one called her work tepid any more. The criticism, rather than depressing her, made her ready to do battle with fury to convert people to the "new poetry." She hired two full-time secretaries. She wrote letters, ran dinner parties, worked on anthologies, lectured, and continued to write poems and give readings. In time, she spoke to audiences of over a thousand people all over America. In all of this Ada helped her. She purchased and borrowed books, organized the household, commented on drafts, corrected galley proofs, and provided emotional support. Her biographer does not address the question of whether they were lovers too. Amy seemed driven in her efforts, as if she knew that she would die young and so had to work faster.

Her anthology, <u>Some Imagist Poets</u>, appeared in 1915 to be followed by several follow-up volumes, the royalties from which Amy delighted in dividing into portions and sending to the authors, some of whom desperately needed money from any source.

Despite her success, Amy could still be hurt by slights and bad reviews. Harriet Monroe omitted Amy in 1916 from a list of prominent poets. The British critics generally disliked her poems and essays and occasionally wrote harsh reviews. Lytton Strachey wrote a sarcastic and cruel piece about her book on French poets. But her resilience and the support of Ada always helped her to recover and rejoin the fray.

There were setbacks. Her stables burnt down in 1909 and the horses killed, possibly a result of arson by enemies of the Lowells (who owned cotton mills in the region), and she turned to raising sheep dogs. (Her brother Lawrence became President of Harvard University that year.)

The summer of 1916 saw, however, a serious accident. After getting her horse carriage stuck in some mud, Amy lifted it out and suffered an umbilical hernia. Lifting a hotel bed later aggravated the condition. From this point on, Amy's health began to deteriorate rapidly. The hernia at first simply added to the problems caused by her gastritis, jaundice and general neurasthenia. By November the pain was so severe that she was given morphine and, in the midst of this, her beloved brother Percy died of a stroke. In September 1918 she had the first of four operations on the hernia, but Amy continued to travel, lecture, write and even do strenuous manual work which often made the recovery from surgery more difficult.

The entry of America into the war in 1917 led to some hardship (though less of course for Amy than for ordinary folk). Her dogs could no longer eat steak, and several died of ptomaine poisoning. However, she laid in so many cigars (ten thousand) that after her death Ada still had many boxes to give away to friends.

Two poets, enemies of Amy's (Witter Bynner and Arthur Ficke) published poems and a manifesto mocking the Imagists, calling themselves the Spectrists. Amy never thought the poems were any good and, when the hoax was revealed, was pleased by her failure to be deceived. However, Bynner began to call Amy the "Hippopoetess," a double insult since, not only did it refer to her obesity, but it also called her a poetess rather than a poet as the modern women preferred to be called. Newspaper columnists began to report anecdotes of Amy which ridiculed her and almost made her into a national joke. In December 1919, Amy was interviewed by the <u>New York Evening Post</u>, and she attacked the press for making fun of everything and described the newspaper columns as ghastly and pitiful. After attacking her comments for a couple of months, the witty columnists stopped making fun of Amy Lowell in their pieces.

Soon after Amy's first operation in 1918, America had several influenza epidemics, and Amy's bout with the flu almost turned into pneumonia. She also developed high blood pressure. In early 1919, her recovery was impeded by the emotional upset from the sudden death of her nephew of meningitis just one day before his boat from Europe was due to dock in New York.

Her eyes began to bother her, and her headaches were diagnosed as resulting from weakness in the retinal muscles. Occasionally, her arguing, which had always been vigorous and spirited, became hysterical, and she would have to apologize for her behavior later. She also began to fear retaliation from the workers against the capitalists, but she never took any steps to ease conditions for workers. Poetry alone was her cause.

She continued to write poems and lectures and to travel to give talks and recitals, and she overstrained herself. The coughing from a cold broke the stitches in December 1919, and she had another operation in early 1920. In March 1920 she found her precious manuscript collection covered in mold and, lifting a pail of water which had been left with them, tore a muscle. That necessitated an operation in October. In April 1921, some stitches seemed loose, and the early summer saw the fourth and final operation. These operations caused a great deal of pain, and most were followed by abscesses.

In the midst of these operations, Amy worked on a book of poems about North American Indians (<u>Legends</u>) and a translation of Chinese poems into English (<u>Fir-Flower Tablets</u>). Critics liked <u>Legends</u> but disapproved of <u>Fir-Flower Tablets</u>.

She next suffered a mild heart attack and retinal hemorrhages. The hernia broke through again, her blood pressure rose to 240, but still she kept working frenetically. In 1922, she determined to finish her biography of Keats, but first she wrote an anonymous spoof of modern poets (including herself), a hoax to which she did not admit for over a year (A Critical Fable). She was upset in 1922 when Edna Millay became the first woman to win a Pulitzer Prize for poetry. (Amy's came posthumously in 1926.) A final lecture tour was completed in January 1923, and then Amy and Ada went to see Eleanor Duse on her return tour to America. Amy did everything she could to make the trip pleasant for the actress (including making sure she had champagne at every stop, a difficult task during these times of Prohibition). Then, just before the actress was due to stay with Amy (for which Amy had the bathroom remodelled), the actress died in April 1924 in Pittsburgh.

The eleven hundred page manuscript on Keats finally reached the publisher in November of that year. That Autumn her brother-in-law died and, in February 1925, her sister Katie fell to her death out of a window in New York City. The biography was released in February to good reviews in America and poor reviews in England where they seemed to be jealous that an American could write a good biography on Keats. (The English critics ignored the fact that more material on Keats was in America than England and that Amy herself had a good collection.)

By March, Amy's weight was down to 160 pounds from a high of 250. (She was only just over five foot tall.) An operation to correct the hernia was scheduled for May but, the day before the operation on May 12, 1925, Amy had a stroke which affected the right side of her body. She died an hour and a half later.

Discussion

Amy appears to have a relatively uneventful childhood and adolescence. She was overweight and lacked female friends. But she was the youngest daughter in a wealthy family, with parents and siblings who loved her. She was happy in those years. Her mother was sickly, and she was raised by a governess. However, this would have been the case whatever the state of her mother's health. There were no major losses in those years.

Amy was disappointed in love and ended up a spinster, a role she did not desire at all. But she made good friends during her life, and her close relationship with Ada for much of her adult life was clearly as close as, if not closer than, a marriage might have been. It is interesting to speculate how Amy would have coped with Ada's death. (Ada lived until 1952.) Amy's relationship with Ada was so close, and Amy seemed so possessive of Ada, resenting even Ada's visits to her own daughter, that it does seem somewhat pathological.

Amy's identification with her father and older brother and her masculine style, combined with her adoration of Ada does suggest homosexual tendencies. We do not know whether she was aware of these tendencies or labelled them as such and whether she actualized them in behavior.

Amy was very eccentric, what with her public cigar smoking, receiving visitors while in bed, and her assertive style with colleagues, editors and audiences. (She would urge audiences to clap or hiss her rather than simply sit there silently.) There were occasions when she took to bed exhausted and despondent. Her fears and paranoia seemed to be growing in intensity as she got older, but there appear to be no signs of serious psychiatric disorder at all. However, had she lived longer, these mild behaviors might well have become more dysfunctional.

Although stung by criticism of her work, Amy would eventually continue with her plans and projects and to challenge her critics. She treated writing more like a business, and she used an assertive (almost bullying) manner to further her aims. Being from a wealthy family made it harder at first to begin her career as a serious poet but, in the end, her wealth enabled her to enjoy life and to pursue actively what she wanted. She could buy Keats's manuscripts, have two secretaries to assist her, and even book extra hotel rooms so as to ensure quiet on her corridor when she visited New York City. Perhaps wealth enables people to stay eccentric whereas poverty leads more easily to psychiatric illness?

Edna St. Vincent Millay[3]

Vincent was born on February 22, 1892, in Rockland, Maine, and given her middle name in honor of the hospital that had taken good care of her mother's brother. Family and intimates usually called her Vincent, though her suitors called her Edna. She had two younger sisters, born in 1893 and 1896.

Vincent's mother, Cora Millay, had studied both piano and voice and dreamt of becoming a singer or writer. She gave her daughters music lessons and encouraged them in the arts. Vincent wrote her first poem when she was nearly five. Her parents had a great deal of friction in their

---

[3] This section is based on Gould (1969).

marriage and, when Vincent was seven, her mother told her father to leave. The father visited the girls regularly, but he seemed more like a friendly relative than a father.

For the next few years, Cora Millay moved her children around quite a bit, mostly in Maine and always in New England, finally settling down in Camden, Maine in 1903. She trained and then worked as a nurse which meant that Vincent was often left in charge of her sisters for days at a time. Vincent was, therefore, forced to assume a leadership role by the age of eleven. She scorned the feminine toys of her sisters and seemed more boy than girl.

Her mother encouraged her daughters' appreciation of the arts. Vincent became an accomplished pianist and began a notebook with her poems at the age of twelve. One birthday gift from her mother was a twenty volume encyclopedia. Vincent had her poems published in the school newspaper and, at the age of fourteen, the children's magazine, St Nicholas, began to accept her poems, eventually awarding her their Gold Badge, given to their best writers. She set the Mother Goose rhymes to music and wrote an operatic version of "Little Boy Blue" when she was thirteen. She read extensively, with Shakespeare and Catullus as a base. At high school, she edited the school newspaper and wrote and acted in several school productions. She had difficulty deciding whether to concentrate on music or writing, but soon after graduation decided on writing.

However, after graduation, Vincent had nowhere to go. There was no money in the family for college, and Vincent stayed home, depressed. Her mother discovered a competition for the hundred best poems of the year, and Vincent entered it. The judges liked her poem and ranked it fourth of the more than ten thousand poems submitted. When the book was published, there was a public outcry that her poem had not been ranked first.

Serendipitously, she read the poem in 1912 at a town festivity and was heard by Caroline Dow, head of the National Training School of the YWCA in New York City. Miss. Dow was so impressed by the poem that she decided to raise the money to send Vincent to college. The poem also impressed established writers, and Vincent received letters from and began a correspondence with two professional contributors to the anthology, Witter Bynner and Arthur Ficke.

Miss Dow called for Vincent in January 1913 to come to New York City to take some preliminary courses, and while there she also met established writers such as Louis Untermeyer and Jessie Rittenhouse. Her writing was accepted by Smart Set and Forum, and Mitchell Kennerly offered to publish a book of her poems.

She arrived at Vassar College in the Fall of 1913, twenty-one and resentful of the restrictions she faced as a freshman at college. After breaking rules and getting into trouble, the President of the college told her that he was never going to expel her but that she had to follow the rules of the college. She agreed to try and, once she had agreed, settled down to enjoy an illustrious career at the college, writing creatively and acting in the college theatricals. She wrote class songs and plays and graduated in June 1917.

The Start of the Career

After graduation, Vincent decided to be a poet but to earn a living by acting. She moved to New York City and was helped by a variety of friends who appreciated her talent. She finally found an acting role in December 1917 in a play put on in Greenwich Village by the Provincetown Players during their Winter stay there. One active member, Floyd Dell, fell in love with Vincent, and another romance developed between Vincent and Arthur Ficke, the married poet who had written to her after her success in the national poetry competition. Vincent and Arthur fell in love and most certainly were lovers before Arthur had to leave for a military mission early in 1918. This affair moved them both and spurred them to write poems about it for many years. However, they did not meet again until 1923, and Vincent experienced great pain over the separation and lack of response from Arthur to her declarations of love.

Although she continued to write and though Kennerly had published her prize-winning poem and, later, her first book of poems, she received no royalties from the sales. Meanwhile she continued to act and write plays for the Provincetown Players in Greenwich Village and, in the summer of 1918, she was joined there by her sisters and mother. Vincent's most steady source of money was obtained for her poems published in Ainslee's Magazine and a series of stories she wrote under the pen name of Nancy Boyd, as well as for occasional poems accepted by other magazines.

Other admirers appeared, including Edmond Wilson and John Bishop, juniors on the staff of Vanity Fair, and soon she was publishing in their magazine. Her book of poems entitled A Few Figs From Thistles in 1920, followed by Second April in 1921, brought Vincent enormous popularity. She was called the poet laureate of the 1920s and the spokesperson for the new woman. However, the books continued to earn her little in the way of royalties. She was invited back to Vassar College to read her poems and was commissioned to write a verse play for the fiftieth anniversary of the alumnae association.

Still despairing of ever seeing Arthur again, she took an assignment as foreign correspondent for Vanity Fair and sailed for Europe in January 1921. She was lonely and homesick there to the point of neurosis. Her sisters were now both married, Arthur had fallen in love with someone else, and she impulsively accepted a proposal of marriage from Arthur's friend Witter Bynner. Luckily perhaps, they decided later that to marry each other would be a mistake.

Receiving an advance at last for one of her novels from a reputable publisher, Vincent paid for her mother to join her in Europe. Arthur, now separated from his wife, arrived in Paris with his new love and met Vincent and her mother. Vincent came down with peritonitis and other afflictions, and she returned to America with her mother early in 1923 physically and emotionally exhausted.

Stability and Success

If 1922 was the low point of Vincent's life, 1923 began her ascent. Her 1922 poems won her the Pulitzer Prize, the first time in the field of poetry that it had been awarded to a woman. Harpers took over as her publisher, reissued her earlier books and published the subsequent ones, ensuring her a regular income for many years for her writing. She also ran into Eugen Boissevain again who was the widower of Inez Milholland, a leading suffragist, and they fell in love. Eugen had emigrated to America from the Netherlands as a young man and ran a prosperous import firm. Within a month they had fallen in love, and they married in July. Vincent had an operation for an intestinal problem soon afterwards but recovered quickly.

Initially, Vincent and Eugen moved into the Holley Hotel on Washington Square in New York City. Her new book of poems, The Harp-Weaver And Other Poems, appeared to favorable reviews, and Vincent was asked to compose and read a sonnet at the unveiling of a memorial to three suffragists in Washington DC.

Eugen, twelve years older than Vincent and with the experience of marriage to a suffragist, was an ideal husband for Vincent. He loved her and provided the protection she had never received from her father. A few years after their marriage, he gave up his business to devote his life to Vincent's career. He bought a house for them in Greenwich Village, planned and often accompanied Vincent on her reading tours, and protected her from unwanted intrusions into her life. Arthur and Gladys married and moved into a house around the corner.

After a belated honeymoon trip to the Far East, Eugen and Vincent returned to America where Harper's brought out a collection of the stories she had written under her pen name (to which she wrote an introduction as herself), and she was invited by Deems Taylor to write the libretto for an opera he had been commissioned to write by the Metropolitan Opera Company for their first American opera. In the Spring of 1925, Vincent and Eugen found a fruit and berry farm in New York just across from the Berkshires and began to fix it up, eventually turning it into a working farm. "Steepletop" remained their home for the next twenty-five years, the rest of their life together. In 1933, they bought a small undeveloped island near Brunswick, Maine, and they spent part of each year there away from all distractions, living quite primitively.

That Summer, she received her first honorary doctorate (from Tufts University and the first of many). But she also began to suffer from severe headaches (often accompanied by spots in front of her eyes) which plagued her from time to time for the rest of her life and which left doctors baffled. She was easily exhausted and often had to spend whole days in bed.

For the next twenty five years, Vincent continued to be productive and popular. Over the years, she grew increasingly concerned with social issues and often wrote poems on these issues, poems which were sometimes rushed and not as good poetry as she could write. Though criticized for this work, Vincent felt that the importance of the social issues excused her hasty writing. She was arrested for protesting the execution of Sacco and Vanzetti in August, 1927, and accused of being a communist. She worked for the Stage Relief Fund, the Writers War Board and the Red Cross. The Second World War stripped Eugen of his income from European investments, and Vincent wrote poems to arouse American feeling against the Nazis.

In 1931, her book of poems in celebration of a love affair was published, <u>Fatal Interview</u>, and there was a great deal of speculation on the identity of Vincent's lover about whom she wrote. Her biographer claims that both Vincent and Eugen felt free to have other lovers, though Eugen seems to have been too devoted to and busy with Vincent to have outside erotic interests.

Vincent continued to make reading tours, often accompanied by Eugen who made the arrangements and protected her from the social stress. Even at Steepletop, Eugen would answer the telephone for her, and sometimes disconnect it for long periods, to protect Vincent from distractions. In the mid 1930s, Vincent began to talk of anxieties about her writing. Letter-writing was hard for her, and the criticism she received for her patriotic writings later in the early 1940s affected her self-confidence. From the 1940s on, financial concerns grew, and Vincent often had to ask her publishers for advances on her books.

In 1936, she fell out of the car one day as it turned a corner, and the injuries affected her arm (including her ability to write and feed herself) intermittently thereafter. Her sister, Kathleen had died suddenly in 1943 (her mother had died in 1931), followed by Vincent's editor at Harpers. In 1944, her overwork, physical illnesses and psychological stress led to a nervous breakdown, and she spent several months in the Doctor's Hospital in New York City. When she came out, she suffered from writer's block.

The following year, Arthur Ficke developed cancer and quickly died. From then on, Vincent and Eugen withdrew even more into Steepletop. Financial circumstances forced them to let go all of the servants but one. Visitors noted that Eugen treated Vincent as if she were a baby and that she responded in kind. Alone, however, she still occasionally showed her wit and intelligence. By 1946, she had recovered some of her strength and was writing again. Harpers now had an arrangement whereby they paid her a monthly sum from her royalties, ensuring a regular income for her.

Then in August, 1949, Eugen developed a lung disease and died. Vincent collapsed after the funeral and spent several weeks back in Doctor's Hospital. She returned to Steepletop alone and continued her life there. She died of a heart attack there on October 19, 1950, alone in the house, sitting on the stairs.

Discussion

Although Vincent lost her father through divorce in her childhood, he continued to play a role, albeit minor, in her life, and the loss does not appear to have been as traumatic for her as the loss by death of the mother of Virginia Woolf or the father of Sylvia Plath.

Vincent suffered a great deal of romantic stress in her early 20s from her affair with and love for Arthur Ficke, but she weathered this stress quite well. However, in common with other women of the period, she suffered from a variety of physical ailments which may possibly have had a psychogenic base in part. Indeed, in 1944 and after her husband's death, her problems in coping increased to such an extent that she entered a clinic for treatment. However, there is no evidence that her disturbance was ever psychotic in nature.

Although her biographer minimizes Vincent's alcohol use, Vincent seems to have abused alcohol, on occasions severely. Gould notes that it was Vincent's reckless drinking that sent her back into the hospital after Eugen's death. She notes that Vincent typically drank before and after giving poetry readings and that Upton Sinclair considered her drinking excessive.

Thus, there is evidence for a mild degree of psychological disturbance in Vincent's life.

Georgia O'Keeffe[4]

Georgia O'Keeffe was born in Sun Prairie, Wisconsin, on November 15, 1887, to Frank and Ida O'Keeffe. She was the second born, with an older brother, and five younger siblings. Her father was Irish and her mother a mix of Dutch and Hungarian. Her parents came from neighboring farms, and her father eventually combined both properties.

Georgia's mother, Ida, was energetic, stern and cold. She supported her children's efforts but expected the best. Little affection was shown, and the children could not remember their parents ever putting their arms around each other. Ida's widowed sister, Jennie, lived with the family too, and she provided warmth and physical affection. The family was thrifty. Material possessions were few, and clothes handed down from child to child.

Georgia was spared the demands placed upon the oldest but managed to dominate the younger children as a benevolent despot. She had a room to herself, and her sisters felt that she was the family favorite. She grew up independent and free-spirited. Georgia started school at five and, like her siblings, helped with chores after school. Ida read a lot to the children, played the piano and had a strong commitment to education. She sent her daughters for instruction in music and drawing, and four of the daughters showed talent for drawing. In eighth grade, Georgia told a friend that she planned to be an artist.

After a year at a Catholic School, Georgia was sent with her older brother in 1902 to live with an aunt in Milwaukee so that they could attend the public high school. Meanwhile, since every male member of Frank O'Keeffe's family had died from tuberculosis, the family decided to move away from Wisconsin to see if a different climate would help Frank survive. They choose Williamsburg, Virginia, but, after the move there, the family fortunes declined. Georgia was enrolled in the Chatham Episcopal Institute which she found very restricting after her year away from home at a public high school. However, she survived there and work on her artistic skills. After graduation, Georgia, now seventeen, went to live with an aunt in Chicago so that she could attend the Art Institute. By February 1906 she was first in her class.

---

[4] This section is based on Robinson (1989).

Early Years

Back home in the summer of 1906, Georgia caught typhoid, and the illness prevented her from returning to Chicago. In September 1907 she went to New York to study at the Art Students League. Unlike the Art Institute in Chicago which had taught classically conventional painting, the Art Students League in New York City embraced modern developments in painting and encouraged individuality in style. Here she realized the conflict she faced if she decided to become an artist. Though there were many female students in the league, few went on to build successful careers since the pressures to marry and to take subservient roles to men were strong. Georgia was tempted but decided to limit her social life and her intimacy with men so that she could become an artist.

Georgia's work won prizes, and she was awarded a scholarship to Amitola, an artist's retreat on Lake George in upstate New York. However, the declining family fortunes in Virginia meant that there was no money for Georgia to spend another year in New York City. She moved to Chicago to work as a free lance illustrator for advertising agencies, a job she disliked. After a year, she came down with measles which gave her an excuse to return home to Virginia where her mother now developed tuberculosis. Georgia decided to give up her plans for a career, but she was asked to fill in for an art teacher at Chatham Episcopal College where she had studied, and she realized that she could combine a career as a teacher and artist.

She signed up for summer courses in art at the University of Virginia in 1912 where her teacher encouraged her in her career goals. She then moved to Amarillo (Texas) to teach art at high school for a year where she developed a reputation as an eccentric. She worked as a teaching assistant the following summer at the University of Virginia and returned to Amarillo. After another summer at the University of Virginia, her aunt gave Georgia money to study at Columbia Teachers College in order to obtain a teacher's degree. She then took a position at Columbia College in South Carolina.

The teaching positions that Georgia accepted took her far from the centers of the art world and, therefore, allowed her to work alone without little guidance from others. She sent some of her work to a friend in New York City, Anita Pollitzer, who showed it to Arthur Stieglitz. Alfred Stieglitz, born in America in 1864, was a leading photographer and a vigorous promoter of modern art, as long as he approved of it. He supported women artists and exhibited their work in the small gallery he ran. He liked Georgia's work, and he and Georgia began to correspond.

A job offer from West Texas Normal College meant that Georgia had to take one final course at Columbia Teachers College, and so she left the college in South Carolina after one semester to go to New York. In May Stieglitz hung in his gallery some of the paintings Georgia had sent to Anita, and they began to discuss art. Although they had met once in 1908, when Georgia was twenty and Alfred was forty-four, and though Georgia visited his gallery regularly in 1914 to see the modern artists whose works he exhibited, they had never spent time together. He had been unhappily married for over twenty years and had one daughter, Kitty.

After Georgia went to Texas to teach, they began an intense correspondence and fell in love by mail. Georgia had been attracted to men before and tempted to marry; an artist whom she met at Amitola, George Dannenberg, a college teacher of Political Science who may have proposed to her in 1916, Arthur Macmahon, and one of the older students at West Texas Normal College.

In May of 1916, Georgia's mother died, and Georgia was deeply depressed for six weeks. Teaching summer school at the University of Virginia helped bring her out of the depression, and she began painting again. Back at the West Texas Normal College, Georgia taught and painted, developing a reputation as an eccentric because of her teaching methods, her personal style and her clothes (she preferred black clothes with a masculine style).

In April 1917, Stieglitz gave Georgia her own show at his gallery. She travelled to New York unannounced to see her show, but Stieglitz had taken it down. He rehung it again just for her and took pictures of her standing by her paintings. Her second year in Texas went less well. She found it hard to paint (she often worked in creative bursts followed by exhaustion and apathy), and she had problems with the community, particularly because of their anti-German attitude once America entered the war and her relationship with the older student. In January 1918, she caught influenza and took a medical leave of absence, recuperating at a friend's house in Texas. Stieglitz suggested she return to New York and, after Georgia had an unpleasant encounter with a neighbor who seemed to have assaultive intent, sent a mutual friend (Paul Strand) down to persuade her to leave Texas. Georgia arrived back in New York in June 1919 and soon was living with Stieglitz.

Life With Alfred

Life with Stieglitz began with intensity. Georgia sent a letter of resignation to Texas and, of course, she and Stieglitz became lovers.

Stieglitz was fascinated by Georgia's face and body and began a photographic study of her which lasted fifteen years. As soon as his wife realized what had happened, she asked Stieglitz to leave, and he moved in with Georgia. Stieglitz's mother summoned the pair to her home at Lake George in upstate New York and took a liking to Georgia. Georgia, however, found the Stielgitzs difficult to be with. There could be as many as twenty people for dinner, and emotional explosions occurred with regularity. Georgia missed her privacy and independence, as well as the open plains of Texas.

Stieglitz's wife was angry at the divorce, and the process dragged on for six years and alienated Stieglitz's daughter, Kitty, from him. Kitty married, and then in 1923, had a son and developed a postpartum depression and schizophrenia. Visits from her father worsened her mental state, and so he stopped visiting. Georgia's family was upset that she was living with an older married Jewish man. Thus, both Georgia and Alfred gave up a lot to be with each other. In that same year, 1918, Georgia's sixty-five year old father fell from a roof and was killed. Her brother Alexis returned from the war with heart and lungs damaged by gas. Yet, the siblings, though scattered over America, remained close and attached to Georgia, except for the oldest, Frank, who was anti-Semitic.

Artistically, Georgia and Alfred were enthusiastic about each other's work, and they stimulated each other. Alfred though was rather conservative and viewed each new development in Georgia's style with alarm. At first they were quite poor. Alfred's brother paid the rent on their apartment, and they frequently ate with Alfred's family. (Since Georgia did not cook, they ate out if they were not dining with others.) Georgia was not used to selling and, thereby, losing her paintings. However, sales were necessary for survival, and Alfred allowed occasional sales of her work. Georgia's reluctance to sell her work and Alfred's high price tags meant that very few of her paintings were sold, which increased their value tremendously over the years. In 1922, one of her paintings sold for $400. Her first solo exhibition was in 1923, and six paintings from her 1927 exhibition sold for seventeen thousand dollars. In 1928, Alfred sold six of Georgia's paintings of flowers for twenty-five thousand dollars! In the 1930s, her paintings sold steadily at around $5,000 each.

Life settled down to a routine in which they spent most of the year in New York City working and summers with the family at Lake George. Alfred hated traveling anywhere else. Georgia began making occasional visits to friends of Alfred's in Maine by herself to escape from the stress of Stieglitz family life. At Lake George, Georgia took possession of one of the farm buildings and had it fixed up as a studio from which all the others were banned.

Georgia wanted to have children, but Alfred was totally opposed to this. He was unwilling to share Georgia with anyone else, and his favorite sister had died in childbirth. The postpartum psychosis of his daughter in 1923 settled the issue.

Georgia's reputation was enhanced by an exhibition in 1921 of Alfred's photographs of her, mainly nude. She became a newspaper personality. The sale of six of her paintings for twenty-five thousand dollars in 1928 also made headlines, and her eccentric personality and life style became well known. In the Roaring Twenties, Georgia dressed plainly, usually wearing a black cape over her clothes when out, and kept her hair in a knot, not in fashion at all!

Alfred eventually turned to photographing other women and having romantic flings with them. Georgia did not always find these episodes easy to bear but never interfered, though she sometimes fled to Maine to escape the stress. Alfred turned sixty in 1924 (Georgia was thirty-seven) and began to be physically frail. Despite the problems of life with Alfred, Georgia was sure of his love for her and her love for him. His divorce was final in 1924, and he married Georgia in December of that year. After shifting apartments for many years, they moved into the Shelton Hotel in the Spring of 1925 and remained there for ten years. This arrangement meant that Georgia had to do no housework, and they ate their meals in the hotel.

Alfred's health slowly worsened. He had kidney problems in 1924 and again in 1926. In 1927, Georgia had a lump removed from her breast that turned out to be benign. In 1928 she had a benign cyst removed.

In 1927, a young married woman, Dorothy Norman, met Alfred and began to help out in the art gallery he ran. Gradually, she took on more and more duties and, in time, a love affair developed between them which lasted until his death. Georgia found this affair more difficult to tolerate than the earlier less intense ones, especially since Norman became his photographic model, his professional associate and his creative protegee.[5] Georgia was often depressed and spent more and more time in Maine during the summers apart from Alfred. In the summer of 1928, she visited her sister in Wisconsin but decided that she could not leave Alfred. Soon after she returned in Alfred in mid-August to a tender reconciliation, he had a heart attack.

From 1929 to until Alfred's death in 1946 at the age of eighty-two, a new pattern developed. Alfred stayed either in New York City or at the family estate at Lake George. Georgia, though, could not tolerate the Stieglitz family at Lake George and had come to dislike New York where Alfred's affair with Dorothy Norman continued. Alfred also insisted on

---

[5] Norman wrote poetry.

deciding on the daily pattern of activity. His intentions were benevolent, for Georgia was still the center of his life, but he stifled her.

Georgia found the solution by going in April 1927 to Santa Fe in New Mexico with a friend (Beck Strand) to visit the artists, including many strong and independent women, who had made the town their home. On this first visit they stayed for part of the time with Mabel Luhan in Taos. Georgia and Alfred wrote almost daily, though never about Dorothy Norman, the cause of the tension between them, and Alfred feared that Georgia would never return. But she returned in August. Once reunited, they seemed happy again though the tensions remained.

Georgia continued to make summer trips to New Mexico, and she appears to have decided that her work was the most important thing in her life, and her marriage to Alfred more important her pain over his affair with Norman.

Interestingly, in 1932, Georgia accepted a commission to paint a powder room at the Radio City Music Hall over Alfred's objections. She began work on the project but argued with the designers and walked off the project, probably because she did not have the nerve to continue on a project which Alfred opposed. After her withdrawal from the project she became seriously depressed and developed psychosomatic symptoms. She developed shortness of breath, chest pains, difficulty in speaking, blinding headaches, chronic fatigue and weeping spells. Eventually neurotic symptoms appeared - hypersensitivity to noise, a morbid fear of water and a fear of crowded streets. Georgia had fallen ill, both physically and psychologically, before under stress - after her year in Chicago, her mother's death and her troubles at West-Texas Normal College. Now she had lost Alfred's love to another woman and yet had not freed herself from her love and dependency upon him. On February 1, 1933, Georgia entered Doctor's Hospital for treatment for her neurosis. While there, her sister Catherine had some of her paintings shown in New York City, and Georgia was enraged. The two sisters were estranged for four years, and Catherine never painted again. Alfred was fearful that his beloved Georgia would go mad as his daughter had, and he lessened his involvement with Norman. Georgia left the hospital on March 24th and went to Bermuda to recuperate. She came back and went to Lake George in June staying there for the rest of the year.

Slowly she recovered, not only her health, but also her self-confidence, helped by the stay there with her of Jean Toomer, a leading black writer. By early 1934, Georgia was painting again, and she again resumed her custom of spending the summers in New Mexico, but now with Alfred's blessing. Each year she would go to Lake George in the Spring to open the house there, spend the summer in New Mexico, and return to Lake George in the Fall to close up the house. Winters in New

York were more tolerable since Alfred's frailty forced him to lead a less hectic social life and because Georgia felt freer to avoid those occasions.

Commissioned in 1936 to paint a large picture by Elizabeth Arden Beauty Salons, Georgia rented a large studio, and she and Alfred moved out of the Shelton Hotel into an apartment. Georgia hired a cook-housekeeper to take of them. The relationship between Georgia and Alfred seemed strong, sure and affectionate. Alfred missed her when she left for New Mexico but was confident that she would return. In 1940, she bought her first house in New Mexico.

Georgia was no longer avant-garde but a painter of stature. She was awarded her first honorary doctorate in 1938, commissioned by Steuben Glass to design works in crystal, named in 1939 as one of the twelve most outstanding women of the previous fifty years, given her first retrospective at the Art Institute of Chicago in 1943 (the first there for a woman) and in 1946 at the Museum of Modern Art in New York City (again the first there for a woman), elected to the National Institute of Arts and Letters in 1949, and membership of the American Academy of Arts and Letters in 1962.

She still suffered occasionally from illnesses. In June of 1939, she had headaches, sinus trouble and insomnia and was ordered to bed for six weeks. In the 1940s, her eyesight began to fail. Alfred was also growing weaker. His heart attack and pneumonia in 1938 delayed Georgia's stay in New Mexico that year. She hired a woman to take care of him when she was away, and she gradually moved the focus of her life to New Mexico, buying a house there and hiring someone there to cook and clean the house. She met Maria Chabot, a young woman of twenty-seven, who became a close friend and who lived with Georgia for part of each year for ten years and who remained a good friend for forty years. In 1945, Georgia bought an old ruined house in Abiquiu and had it renovated as her home for the rest of her life.

Alfred died on July 13, 1946, after a stroke. Within days, Georgia removed Dorothy Norman from all involvement with Alfred's projects. Alfred's will named Georgia as his primary heir and executrix, and it took her three years to settle the estate, organize exhibitions, and dispose of Alfred's works (both his own and those of others which he had collected). She engaged a young woman, Doris Bry to help her, and eventually Doris became Georgia's agent in New York City. In 1949, at the age of sixty-two, Georgia moved to New Mexico for good.

Final Years In New Mexico

As soon as she arrived, her friendship with Maria Chabot soured, and Georgia decided to reduce her intimate involvements. Such relationships carried risk as well as rewards. Although an outsider in the town of Abiquiu, Georgia tried to fit in. She built a gymnasium, contributed $50,000 for a new building at the school, paid for clean drinking water, loaned her car to the local baseball team, and helped some of the local children. Her sister Claudia began to visit each summer and took responsibility for the garden. Georgia now could have pets, and she began with kittens and Chow puppies. A local woman, Jerrie Newsom, was cook, housekeeper and companion to Georgia from 1966 to 1974.

Now she could travel, and she took a trip abroad every year until she was ninety-six, beginning with Mexico in 1951, Europe in 1953, Peru in 1956 and around the world in 1959. Her paintings continued to sell well (Doris Bry continued the tradition of selling few and then mainly to museums or to private individuals who promised to give them to museums), and her investments were profitable. In the 1950s and 1960s when the value of Georgia's paintings dropped, Bry bought some back, and then Georgia's popularity returned in the 1970s. (Georgia occasionally had given paintings to friends, but on their death she always requested their return and, surprisingly, got them back!)

In the 1960s, a friend from her days at Columbia Teachers College, Anita Pollitzer worked on an authorized biography, but Georgia eventually refused permission to have it published. This contributed to the mystery about Georgia since so little was known about her life. Although Georgia's closest friends were women, she refused to get involved in feminist issues, refusing even to meet with Gloria Steinem when Steinem traveled to Abiquiu.[6]

Georgia's central vision began to deteriorate in the early 1970s. Then in 1973, a young man knocked at her door to ask whether he could work for her. Juan (John) Hamilton was twenty-six, divorced and rather aimless in his life. He began by doing odd jobs around the house and garden, but slowly became her indispensable companion, despite the fact that the housekeeper quit because of his presence. Even the town residents disliked him. Yet Georgia needed a companion and someone who would do the tasks which now were beyond her. And the dependency was mutual, for Juan became as dependent psychologically and financially on Georgia as she was on him.

Since to see Georgia, you had to go through Juan, people began to accord Juan respect. He worked in ceramics, and Georgia encouraged his work, often forcing people to buy and show his work if they wanted hers. Many of her friends and colleagues resented Juan's influence over

---

[6] Georgia's close friends denied that she ever had sexual relationships with women.

Georgia, but none were willing to take over his role as companion to an almost totally blind and very frail woman. Bry resigned as Georgia's agent because of friction with Juan and sued for thirteen million dollars in damages.[7]

Although Juan married in 1980 and had his own place, Georgia seemed to grow increasingly dependent upon him and, friends thought, even in love with him. Their relationship continued to cause tension in her relationship with her sister Claudia and other friends. However, some observers noticed the affection Juan showed to Georgia and the undeniable support and assistance he gave her. He helped her complete her autobiography in 1976, and in 1978 he was given power of attorney over her affairs.

By 1982, Georgia was ninety-five, very frail, nearly blind and quite deaf. In 1984 Claudia died, and Georgia had a heart attack. Juan had Georgia moved to a house in Santa Fe so that he could take better care of her. She changed her will that year, leaving almost everything to Juan. For the next year-and-a-half, Georgia stayed in her bedroom, facing the window, saying little. A nurse was on constant duty, and Juan visited in the morning and evening. She seemed peaceful and otherworldly. She died on March 6, 1986 at the age of ninety-eight.

Georgia's family challenged the will, and a settlement was arranged based on an earlier will from 1979.

Discussion

Georgia had a secure and stable childhood which prepared her well for life's stresses. Her marriage, though it fulfilled many of her needs, also caused her a great deal of pain. Despite a brief neurotic episode, Georgia found the strength to build a healthy life in which she could satisfy both her need for creative work and her need for a meaningful relationship with her husband. She coped well with the death of her husband, prepared for his death by her growing independence from him over the years and now doing those things which had been difficult for her during her marriage. In old age and senility, she was able to form interpersonal bonds with people willing to take care of her, even though some relatives and friends thought that she was abused.

---

[7] She settled for much less than this sum.

References

Gould, J. <u>The poet and her book</u>. New York: Dodd, Mead, 1969.
Gould, J. <u>Amy</u>. New York: Dodd, Mead, 1975.
Lottman, H. <u>Colette</u>. Boston: Little Brown, 1991.
Robinson, R. <u>Georgia O'Keeffe</u>. New York: Harper & Row, 1989

Chapter 6

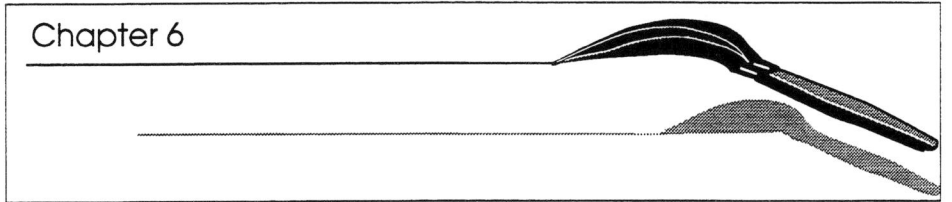

COMPARING THE SUICIDAL AND NONSUICIDAL WOMEN

We have presented the lives of six creative women who committed suicide and six who died natural deaths. In this chapter we will explore whether clear differences are apparent between the two groups.

First some simple demographic information.

Name	Birth	Death	Age	Birthorder[1]
Diane Arbus	Mar. 14, 1923	Jul. 26, 1971	48	2nd of 3
Dora Carrington	Mar. 29, 1893	Mar. 11, 1932	38	4th of 5
Sylvia Plath	Oct. 27, 1932	Feb. 11, 1963	30	1st of 2
Anne Sexton	Nov. 9, 1928	Oct. 4, 1973	44	3rd of 3
Sara Teasdale	Aug. 8, 1884	Jan. 30, 1933	48	4th of 4
Virginia Woolf	Jan. 25, 1882	Mar. 28, 1941	59	3rd of 4
Colette	Jan. 28, 1873	Aug. 3, 1954	81	2nd of 2
Käthe Kollwitz	July 8, 1867	Apr. 22, 1945	77	3rd of 4
Amy Lowell	Feb. 9, 1874	May 12, 1925	51	4th or 4
Edna Millay	Feb. 22, 1892	Oct. 19, 1950	58	1st of 3
Georgia O'Keeffe	Nov. 15, 1887	Mar. 6, 1986	98	2nd of 7
Dorothy Parker	Aug. 22, 1893	Jun. 7, 1967	73	3rd of 3

---

[1] For surviving children and excluding half-siblings

Rather obviously, the suicides died at an earlier age than those dying of natural causes. This premature death has been noted before for samples of female and male writers who were alcoholics (Davis, 1986) and writers who committed suicide (Lester, 1991). No differences were noted in birth order, though Lester (1987) concluded from a review of research on this factor that suicides were more often first-borns and middle-borns and less often last-borns. Finally, only one of the women

	Marital Status	Children	Parental Death
Diane Arbus	Divorced	2	none
Dora Carrington	Single	0	none
Sylvia Plath	Separated	2	Father, 8, Natural
Anne Sexton	Divorced	2	none
Sara Teasdale	Divorced	0	none
Virginia Woolf	Married (1st)	0	Mother, 13, Natural
Colette	Married (3rd)		none
Käthe Kollwitz	Widowed		none
Amy Lowell	Single		none
Edna Millay	Widowed		Father, 7, Divorce
Georgia O'Keeffe	Widowed		One
Dorothy Parker	Widowed		Mother, Infancy, Natural

(Dora Carrington) died within a month of her birth, indicating little evidence, therefore, for a "birthday blues" phenomenon (Lester, 1986).

Only five of the eight married women had children, and only two were married at the time of their death. Four of the six suicides were divorced or separated versus none of the nonsuicidal women. Four of the latter were widowed versus none of the suicides. In one case (Sylvia Plath) the separation appear to play a major role in the suicide. For three others (Diane Arbus, Anne Sexton and Sara Teasdale) divorce left them quite lonely and isolated, and all three seem to have been worse off psychologically after the divorce although all three had initiated their divorces.

Though early parental loss is often associated with suicide later in life (Lester, 1992), only two of the suicides and one of the natural deaths had lost a parent through death. Among these losses, the writer who seemed to be most obviously affected by it was Sylvia Plath, whose writings indicate that her suicide was motivated in part by reunion fantasies toward her loved/hated father.

Suicides are often found to have made prior nonfatal suicidal actions.[2] Four of the suicidal women had made prior nonfatal suicidal actions (Dora Carrington, Sylvia Plath, Anne Sexton and Virginia Woolf). Interestingly, all switched methods for their final fatal suicidal action, an unusually high percentage (Clarke and Lester, 1989). Apart from Dora Carrington, the remaining three women who had a history of nonfatal suicidal behavior had been suicidal for a long period in their lives. Research indicates that those who make nonfatal suicidal actions are at higher risk for subsequent fatal suicide. Dorothy Parker made two nonfatal suicidal actions early in her life but died at the age of 73 of natural causes. Thus, four of the five women who made nonfatal suicidal actions subsequently killed themselves.

Name	Method used	Prior attempts/age
Diane Arbus	barbiturates	none
Dora Carrington	gun	car exhaust/38
Sylvia Plath	domestic gas	poison/20
Anne Sexton	car exhaust	several overdoses
Sara Teasdale	poison	none
Virginia Woolf	drowning	jumping 22/poison/31

---

[2] The usual terms for these behaviors (attempted suicide and completed suicide) have been rejected as sexist since they imply that the behavior most common in men (completed suicide) is a successful behavior whereas the behavior most common in women (attempted suicide) is a failure. I have chosen to use the terms "nonfatal" and "fatal" suicide behavior/actions instead (Canetto and Lester, 1993).

There is good evidence for alcohol and drug abuse in Anne Sexton (a suicide) and alcohol abuse in Edna Millay and Dorothy Parker (both natural deaths). Though research has shown that suicide is more common in drug and alcohol abusers, and though some theorists (for example Menninger [1938]) see alcohol and drug abuse as a form of suicide, *chronic suicide*, substance abuse does not appear to be relevant in the present sample of suicidal writers.

Perhaps the most startling results come when we look at the psychiatric disorders of the writers. Of course, diagnosis after a person is dead is an unreliable process. However, there is evidence of a major affective disorder in four of the suicidal women versus none of the nonsuicidal women. Three of the suicides had received psychiatric treatment (Diane Arbus, Sylvia Plath, Anne Sexton), and two were psychiatrically hospitalized (Sylvia Plath and Anne Sexton). Virginia Woolf's affective disorder seems to have been bipolar (a manic-depressive disorder), and Sylvia Plath's disorder may also have been bipolar (Brian Barraclough, personal communication). Depression was also characteristic of Sara Teasdale, though an accurate diagnosis of her psychiatric condition is not possible. In contrast, none of the nonsuicidal women appears to have been chronically depressed or to have had an affective disorder.

Name	Psychiatric disorder
Diane Arbus	Depressive Disorder
Dora Carrington	None
Sylvia Plath	Depressive Disorder
Anne Sexton	Depressive Disorder/ Hysteric Neurosis/ Substance Abuse
Sara Teasdale	Depressed Mood
Virginia Woolf	Depressive Disorder
Colette	None
Käthe Kollwitz	None
Amy Lowell	None
Edna Millay	Alcohol Abuse
Georgia O'Keeffe	Neurosis (Anxiety Disorder)
Dorothy Parker	Alcohol Abuse

Recently, Andreasen (1987) has published a study of thirty faculty at the writers' workshops at the University of Iowa. Of these, 30 percent were judged to be abusing alcohol and 80 percent to have an affective disorder (both figures much higher than for a comparison group of nonwriters). None of the writing faculty were schizophrenic, but two had already committed suicide by the time of the published report of the study.

Andreasen also studied the first-degree relatives of the writers and the comparison group. The relatives of the writers had a higher incidence of affective disorder (in both the parents and the siblings of the writers), but no differences in the incidence of alcoholism. Three of the first-degree relatives of the writers had committed suicide as compared to none of the comparison group's relatives.

Andreasen found also that the relatives of the writers had significantly more creative siblings than the relatives of the comparison group. (The writers and comparison group did not differ in intelligence test scores.)

Andreasen concluded that writing creativity and affective disorder were clearly associated and may have a genetic basis. Andreasen's results are consistent with a study by Kay Jamison on British writers who also had a high incidence of affective disorder (Holden, 1987). A study underway by Hagop Akiskal has revealed that patients with moderately severe affective disorder have a higher incidence of creativity (Holden, 1987).

Holden noted that many of the patients with affective disorder appear to have a bipolar variant, with periods of depression and mania. This is perhaps true of some of the writers discussed in this book, such as Sylvia Plath and Virginia Woolf who appeared to have had periods of remarkable energy and enthusiasm. Creative episodes have similarities to mild levels of mania, both being characterized by high energy, a sensitivity to internal and external stimuli, a breakdown of intellectual inhibitions permitting more creative work, and an unusually good ability to concentrate. Holden concluded that a tendency toward bipolar affective disorder may facilitate creativity.

The Role that Creativity Played

Being a creative artist involves a couple of risks that most people do not take. First, this intensely personal document that you produce (photograph, picture, poem, essay or novel) must be submitted to others for acceptance. Few writers have never suffered a rejection. Most endure many, many rejections before work is accepted. This rejection is not merely a minor setback in a career. It is a rejection of this intensely personal product.

Second, artistic productions are reviewed by critics. Reviews are often critical. After all, a critic who praises everything without qualification would never receive acclaim as a reviewer! Critics have to be negative. Even when praising a work they think highly of, they typically find some small area to criticize.

We have seen in the biographies above how the women were affected by the reception their work received. Of the six suicides, Dora Carrington appears to have lost confidence in her ability as a painter, Sylvia Plath had just published her first novel to luke-warm reviews, Sara Teasdale was experiencing severe writer's block, and Virginia Woolf was acutely anxious in the time leading up to publication of her novels and depressed afterwards. Diane Arbus and Anne Sexton seemed least affected by their creative careers.

Despite these difficulties with their artistic careers, the suicides seem to have been motivated in addition by other factors. For example, Sylvia Plath's suicide seems to be determined more by her chronic depression, her attachment to her deceased father, and the break-up of her marriage than by her career.

Sara Teasdale was finding it hard to write again. Poems did not flow easily any more, and a biography of Christina Rossetti was floundering. However, more important in understanding her suicide was her failure to develop a satisfying marriage and her ensuing loneliness, her chronic depression, and her growing, unfounded fear of a catastrophic physical illness.

Although Virginia Woolf suffered from acute anxiety during the preparation of each novel and depression after the publication, and although her work was no longer held in such high esteem as she grew older, her suicide seems primarily motivated by her fear of her continual depressions. Her suicide seems to be an escape from the unbearable psychological torment she experienced when depressed.

Did Writing Help or Harm the Suicidal Women?

The question has been asked whether writing is (or can be) therapeutic for creative writers or whether it is a stressor which contributes to their psychological disturbance.

Silverman and Will (1986) analyzed the life and suicide of Sylvia Plath and concluded that, although she tried to control her suicidal impulses by means of her poetry, she failed in this endeavor. Silverman and Will argued that poetry is successful when it bridges the inner worlds of the creative person and the audience. (We presume that they mean critically successful, for even poor poetry can serve a useful psychological function for the writer, even if it is merely cathartic.) To be successful, poetry must first achieve a balance between the writer's use of the audience to serve his or her own narcissistic needs (a type of exhibitionism) and the desire to give others a way of structuring the terrors and anxieties that afflict us all (a homonomous desire on the part of the writer to use a term coined by Andras Angyal [1965]).

The writer must also achieve a balance between the potentially destructive conscious and unconscious forces motivating the writing and the constructive desires to harness these forces for the purpose of writing creatively. Related to this, the writer must balance primary and secondary process mechanisms. The writer must also compromise between the fantasy permissible in writing and the acceptance of reality necessary for successful living.

When they apply their ideas to Sylvia Plath, Silverman and Will assert that the successful creative process is successful only when the unconscious forces in the writer operate silently and remain hidden from view. This assertion represents a rather traditional view of creative writing. It would seem to express a preference on the part of Silverman and Will for a particular type of literature rather than expressing a universal truth. For example, the unconscious forces motivating Ernest Hemingway may be under control in his writing, but they are certainly not hidden. More pertinently, the confessional style of poetry developed by W. D. Snodgrass and Robert Lowell and pursued by Anne Sexton is in direct opposition to Silverman and Will's view.

Silverman and Will see the transitional period in Plath's poetry as being her final years in the United States. Plath may have had her confidence undermined by the frequent rejections that writers must endure so that she changed her style. In her new style, she revealed her deepest feelings in her poems, using her experiences to create the poem rather than to simply transform it. Silverman and Will note that she described her early poems as "proper in shape and number and every part" but not alive. Her poems moved from being a reordering and reshaping of experience with a poetic purpose toward becoming expressions of herself. She identified with her poems, which made their rejection even more painful, and Silverman and Will label this change as a "narcissistic regression."

The causal sequence which Silverman and Will propose for Plath has no evidence for or against it. It is simply one reading of Plath's life. Other, equally plausible, alternative paths can be proposed. For example, it is quite likely that Plath's participation, along with Anne Sexton with whom she became very close, in a poetry workshop run by Robert Lowell had a major impact on her writing style. Several members of his workshop adopted a more self-revealing content for their poems, and two received Pulitzer prizes for their work (Lowell and Sexton).

Furthermore, Plath, as she herself clearly recognized, was prone to recurring depressions. In all probability, Plath had an affective disorder, possibly bipolar, and her depressions were likely to reoccur periodically. It is evident from the severity of her depression in 1953 which led to a very serious suicide attempt that she would likely become suicidal again with each new depression (much as Virginia Woolf had).

What is interesting is that, whereas in the early 1950s, her writing may not have helped her cope with the stressors, external and intrapsychic, with which she was confronted, in the later 1950s her switch to a more revealing and personalized style of writing may have helped her survive. Silverman and Will claimed that her writing failed to prevent her suicide. I suggest that it may have postponed her suicide.

In the months prior to her suicide, Plath wrote feverishly, sometimes producing several poems in one day. (We see this feverish activity in the months prior to a suicide also in Anne Sexton.) What would Silverman and Will suggest as a more appropriate strategy for a person confronting intrapsychic turmoil who is not under professional care? It is very likely that the writing helped Plath control her inner turmoil, and some commentators think that the poems she produced were among her finest.

In seeking to formulate a _general_ hypothesis about the role of writing for the depressed and distressed person, it is obviously important to discuss more than one case. In the present context, the life and suicide of the poet Anne Sexton is relevant.

Lester and Terry (1992) argued that writing poetry can be useful with suicidal clients. Writing poems _per se_ may not be helpful to the client, but the revision of the initial drafts of poems may be therapeutically useful. Revising poems may serve a similar function for clients as the journal assignments devised by cognitive therapists by giving the clients intellectual control over their emotions and distance from the traumatic memories.

Sexton revised her poems extensively and, in the process of revision, had to concentrate on form rather than content. This allows for both the action that therapists deem to be therapeutic and the distancing of the self from one's problems. Because Sexton ultimately chose the moment of her death, one should not discount the therapeutic help her writing afforded her.

Anne Sexton illustrates the dialectic in poetry as therapy, between expression and catharsis on the one hand and cognitive control on the other. For Sexton, as long as she was able to stay psychiatrically stable, she was able to apply the craft of poetry to her creative productions. Both Sexton and Martin Orne, her first therapist, believed that her poetry had helped her recover. Only toward the end of her life, as her ability to craft her poems declined, so did her mental stability dissipate.

Interestingly, both Plath and Sexton showed manic trends prior to their suicides, writing poems furiously, poems with more emotional expression and less poetic crafting. Rather than arguing that writing poetry contributed in part to their suicides, it makes much more sense to say that, in their final breakdowns, poetry was no longer able to help them deal with the intrapsychic forces driving them as it had in the past. As their inner turmoil increased, both wrote feverishly, almost like a safety valve letting out the steam under pressure in a boiler, but to no avail since the pressure was building up faster than they could release it.

But this final failure of the craft of poetry to keep Sylvia Plath and Anne Sexton alive does not, as Silverman and Will argue, signify total failure. Both were outstanding poets and functioned quite well given their probable affective disorders. I would argue that the craft of poetry kept both poets alive for many years after their self-destructive impulses first manifested themselves and so signifies success.

Conclusions

It is clear that depression, both of psychiatric proportions and of moderate intensity, played a role in all of the suicides committed by the writers discussed in this book.

It is clear also that for two of the women their fear of being unable to continue to be successful writers played an important role in their suicides. Sara Teasdale and Virginia Woolf feared that their work would never be held in as high esteem as it once was or that they would never be able to write again.

The life of a creative person is not easy. The public exposure of one's innermost thoughts and feelings is hard to endure, and the literary and public reaction to one's work is fraught with potential hurt. When a writer is plagued by severe depression and beset with interpersonal difficulties, it is even harder to develop the resources to withstand the criticism, learn from it or ignore it. Then, the criticism feeds into one's own self-doubts so deeply that it is hard to maintain the self-confidence to continue. Only those with low aspirations or a secure sense of self and with friends and loved ones to support them can withstand the pressure.

References

Angyal, A. Neurosis and treatment. New York: Wiley, 1965. Andreasen, N. C. Creativity and mental illness. AmericanJournal of Psychiatry, 1987, 144, 1288-1292.

Canetto, S., & Lester, D. (Eds.) Women and suicide. New York: Springer, 1993.

Clarke, R. V., & Lester, D. Suicide: closing the exits. New York: Springer-Verlag, 1989.

Davis, W. M. Premature mortality among prominent American authors noted for alcohol abuse. Drug & Alcohol Dependence, 1986, 18, 133-138.

Holden, C. Creativity and the troubled mind. Psychology Today, 1987, 21(4), 9-10.

Lester, D. The birthday blues revisited. Acta Psychiatrica Scandinavica, 1986, 73, 322-323.

Lester, D. Suicide and sibling position. Individual Psychology, 1987, 43, 390-395.

Lester, D. Premature mortality associated with alcoholism and suicide in American writers. Perceptual & Motor Skills, 1991, 73, 162.

Lester, D. Why people kill themselves. Springfield, IL: Charles Thomas, 1992.

Lester, D., & Terry, R. The use of poetry therapy. *The Arts in Psychotherapy*, 1992, 19, 47-52.

Menninger, K. *Man against himself*. New York: Harcourt Brace & World, 1938.

Silverman, M. A., & Will, N. P. Sylvia Plath and the failure of emotional self-repair through poetry. *Psychoanalytic Quarterly*, 1986, 55, 99-129.

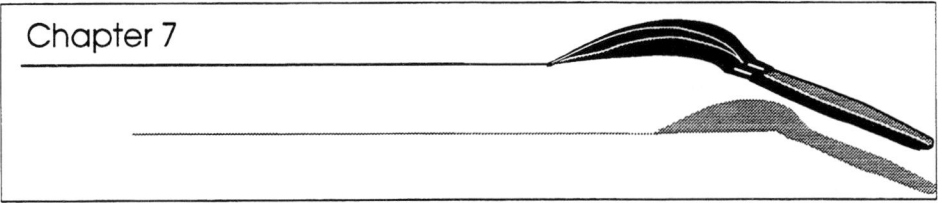

SIX CREATIVE MEN WHO COMMITTED SUICIDE

So far we have compared the lives of six creative women who committed suicide with six creative women who died of natural causes. The next question we shall address is whether the lives of suicidal creative women differ from the lives of suicidal creative men. In this chapter we will present the lives of six creative men who killed themselves and in the final chapter (Chapter 8) compare the lives of the suicidal women and men.

There are many creative men who have committed suicide and with full biographies available to choose from for this book. Of the writers, four were chosen (John Berryman, Hart Crane, Vachel Lindsay and Cesare Pavese). The two modern (Twentieth Century) painters who have committed suicide for whom biographies have appeared (Mark Gertler and Mark Rothko) were also chosen, providing four writers and two artists to match the creative suicidal women.

John Berryman[1]

John Berryman was an American poet, winner of the Pulitzer Prize and other literary awards, who jumped to his death in 1972, at the age of 57. I have relied on the biography written by Haffenden (1982) for this section.

---

[1] This section is based on Haffenden (1982).

Early Life

John was born on October 25, 1914, in McAlester, Oklahoma. His mother Martha was from a Southern family. Her father deserted the family when she was five, and she never felt that her mother loved her. Martha was working as a school teacher in Sasakwa, Oklahoma, when she met John Allyn Smith, a bank manager in McAlester. (John Allyn was born in Minnesota.) They married in July, 1912, when Martha was eighteen and John was twenty-five.

It is not clear whether Martha loved John Allyn, but they kept up appearances. The first child, later known as John Berryman, was born by cesarean operation, and Martha felt that her sins had prevented her from the agony experienced in a normal birth! She felt incomplete without suffering pain. When she was pregnant again, both her husband and her mother wanted her to have an abortion. They feared for her life, and her husband was not sure he could afford two children. Robert was born, however, in 1919.

John's childhood began uneventfully. John was raised as a Catholic, and the family was devout. He felt some sibling rivalry when his brother was born. John later remembered an incident when he pushed Robert off a wall and bloodied him.

In 1924, John's father had trouble at his bank. Perhaps there was rivalry with a colleague; perhaps he neglected his duties? At any rate, the family moved to Florida. Martha and John Allyn had also been having marital problems, perhaps because of Martha's intense attachment to her children. John Allyn also had at least one affair of which Martha was aware.

At first, just Martha, John Allyn and Martha's mother moved to Florida, leaving the two boys in a boarding school. However, the boys were bullied and unhappy there and soon joined their parents. Their father bought a restaurant and also worked as a real estate salesman. This was the time of the Florida land boom, which soon ended, leaving people with land worth much less than they paid for it. In 1926, John Allyn sold the restaurant for a third of what he had paid, and the family moved into an apartment building owned by John Angus Berryman.

It was soon obvious that Martha and John Angus were attracted to each other. John Allyn was distressed over his career crisis and had an affair with a Cuban woman. He asked Martha for a divorce so that he could marry his lover, and she agreed. Because of his distress, Martha had encouraged John Allyn to consult with psychiatrists, but these visits did not seem to help. It is possible that John Allyn considered drowning himself with his son Robert, but regardless of the truth of this report it is clear that John Allyn was very disturbed by his life situation.

In the period leading up to John Allyn's suicide, he was having arguments with Martha and John Angus, he remained unemployed, and his Cuban mistress went back to Cuba leaving him without any money. His divorce was to be finalized on June 26th, and on June 25th Martha suggested continuing their marriage. John Allyn refused and shot himself with a .32 automatic pistol early in the morning of June 26th. (Incidentally, John Allyn's elder sister had also killed herself.)

In later years, John Berryman called his father's suicide the turning point in his life, a turning point toward psychological instability. His biographer saw the father's suicide as a convenient rationalization for John. John felt guilt over his father's death and also anger. His father's death also threw him even more to his mother and her overpossessive love.

Within a few months of John Allyn's death Martha married John Angus (in September 1926), and her sons took his name. John Angus was forty-eight, and Martha was now thirty-two. The family moved to New York City where John Angus was a bond salesman. The family switched also to the Episcopalian faith. Again, it is not clear whether Martha loved John Angus.

In New York City, John, now twelve years old, went to public school, but two years later he went to South Kent School, a private school in Connecticut. John was bullied there and very unhappy but made good academic progress. The school affected a disdain for academic pursuits and stressed athletic prowess of which John had little. John was withdrawn, unaggressive, physically inept and wore glasses with thick lenses which earned him the nickname of 'Blears'. His mother, who earlier had encouraged John's interest in literature, pushed him to succeed in both academics and athletics, adding to his conflict.

John was sick a lot during these school years. He worried about his complexion and dandruff, and his concern over his hair loss and itching scalp continued into adulthood. In March 1931, John encountered three schoolmates by the railroad track who began to torment him. John threw himself in front of an oncoming train but was dragged away by the other boys. Despite this early suicide attempt, John did not attempt suicide again before his death, although he often wrote about suicide in his diary.

John became the foremost scholar at his school, with an average in the nineties, twenty one points above the school average. His mother continued to encourage his interest in literature, actively engaging in discussions with him about books. He wrote for the school newspaper and became the first boy at the school to bypass the sixth form and enter college from the fifth form.

Interestingly, the love and attention from his mother made his vacations in New York City very different from his bleak existence at school. In New York City, he was fashionably dressed, a flirt with girls, a good dancer, and a theater and film enthusiast. But it is questionable how self-confident John really felt in New York City since his later life shows much evidence of his lack of self-confidence and his inability to cope with the stresses of day-to-day life.

John Angus's health eventually began to fail, and Martha began to work more (in the world of fashion and advertising), eventually becoming the major provider for the family. There were hard times, however. John's brother was withdrawn from South Kent School, and John needed a scholarship to attend Columbia University.

During his freshman year at Columbia, John was academically unmotivated and over-involved with social activities. He pursued dancing, music, chess, theater, bridge, and tennis. He usually had a girl friend and would get upset whenever one of these relationships ended. On some occasions he would talk of suicide while distraught over these break-ups.

Because John had flunked an English course, he lost his scholarship and was obliged to drop out for a semester. As he moved through Columbia, his amorous adventures and traumas continued, though he remained a virgin, but his interest in literature gradually grew. He began to draft poems which were published in Columbia Review and came under the influence of a professor there, Mark Van Doren. He graduated in 1936 Phi Beta Kappa, after a crisis over a C in one course which would have prevented his graduation. (John had taken a dislike to the instructor.) He won a fellowship to study at Cambridge University. However, his excessive study, staying up all night at times, led to exhaustion which was complicated by a bad ear infection. Doctors advised Martha to withdraw John from college, but John continued to work and passed.

As we leave this early phase of John's life, two themes emerge from the college years. First is John's need for women in his life and his distress when the relationships fail. Eventually we shall see how John's relationships with women became critical in his life. Second, once John decided to apply himself to his studies, he overdid it. Working throughout the night to the point of exhaustion became a general pattern in his life and he seems driven. Women, work and breakdown characterize most of John's later life.

His Career

John's career involved many moves and he was often unemployed or appointed only for temporary positions (weeks or months at a time). Thus, he faced job insecurity for much of his life. He studied for two years in England and returned to the USA in 1938 where he remained unemployed for a year. He spent one year as an instructor at Wayne State University, three years at Harvard University, and eight years in various capacities at Princeton University where he taught occasionally and was supported by fellowships. In 1954, John was appointed to teach at the University of Iowa, but he was dismissed after a drunken altercation. In 1955, he began teaching at the University of Minnesota, and he remained there for the rest of his life, eventually becoming a Regent's Professor of Humanities in 1969. Interspersed throughout this career were several sabbatical leaves.

Much of this career involved uncertainty. Though John was awarded many prizes and fellowships which helped support him and his family, he was turned down for others and lived with the uncertainty each time he applied for a fellowship as to whether it would be awarded him. He was in financial straits for much of his life, except toward the end, and never owned a house until after his third marriage. (He finally bought a house in Minneapolis in 1964.)

John's work never was easy. His first teaching position was at Wayne State University, where he sank into a cycle of alienation, bouts of work, followed by starvation and social withdrawal. Although college teaching is a relative easy job, many college teachers work themselves into exhaustion and mental breakdowns, and John was one of those teachers who broke down. For example, at Wayne State University John assigned lots of papers to his students and then decided that he had to read each paper carefully and write voluminous comments. When the pile of unread papers grew too great, John would spend hours at a time without a break for food or relaxation in order to read them. At this time too, his fiancé was in England, and they were growing apart.

His Poetry and Essays

John's writing was the dominant activity in his life. He wrote as if compelled to work through on paper the conflicts in his mind. His poems were intensely personal. For example, his sonnets, published in 1967, were written in 1947 to his mistress with whom he was in love (a married woman, Lise).

Throughout his life, John was productive, getting his poems and critical essays published quite successfully. However, writing inevitably involves many rejections too. No one escapes them. The rejections upset John terribly, probably because of his doubts about his own merits as a writer. As his career progressed, the honors came faster: Rockefeller Fellowships, Guggenheim Fellowships, a Pulitzer Prize, and so on. However, as his career progressed, his aspirations increased. Once it was enough to have his poems accepted for publication. Then the books of poems had to be praised, and finally he needed to be the greatest living American poet. What would have once thrilled him soon ranked as a bitter disappointment because of what he did not achieve. Toward the end of his life, John doubted more and more the quality of his work, and he sought the praise of his friends for his latest poems after each draft.

His Marriages

John married three times, but there were numerous other loves and sexual conquests. He had a number of 'loves' while at Columbia, and but his first serious involvement was with a 'Beatrice' in England (about whom the biographer tells us little), two years John's junior. They were engaged to marry, although they had doubts about their relationship. John's return to the USA in 1938 introduced strains into the relationship, particularly since John had by no means freed himself from his mother's possessive love. Beatrice visited John in October 1938, staying until April 1939. She felt that John was not serious about finding a job (they could not live on the proceeds from his writing), and she disapproved of the pattern of his life. (After she returned to England, John had an affair that he told her about, forcing her to 'forgive' him.) She promised to wait until 1941 for John to get his life in order, but the Second World War intervened. (Beatrice decided to stay in England for the duration of the war.) However, it is unlikely that they would have married even had there been no war. During his first teaching position, at Wayne State University, John began sleeping with his students, and this became typical for him throughout his career.

After moving to Harvard University, John met Eileen Mulligan who had been a friend of one of John's girl friends at Columbia University and who had read his letters back then. They met in 1941 and became engaged in July 1942, just after Beatrice wrote to break off her engagement to John. They married in October.

The marriage seems to have been tolerable given that few people could have been happy with a person like John. However, in 1947, John fell in love with a twenty-seven year old married friend, Lise, and spent the summer writing sonnets about her and trying to persuade her to make love "just one more time." The affair was over by the end of the year, leaving John with a memory of ecstasy and a lot of guilt. Lise refused to leave her husband, which is perhaps as well for John, for it is by no means clear that he could have left Eileen. John turned to thoughts of suicide again but began seeing a psychiatrist in order to understand himself better.

Although John and Eileen stayed married, John threw himself into alcohol and affairs. His targets were mainly young married women, and his sexual desires so strong that he often masturbated after being with a lover. By 1949, his day was also filled with drug use including vitamins, an anti-spasmodic, dexedrine, martinis, nembutal and sherry. All this while smoking heavily!

Eileen had serious back problems following a fall, which brought out John's lack of concern for her. She also pursued a career, earning a Masters degree and working as a clinical psychologist. By 1953, Eileen had suffered enough from John's neglect, infidelities, drug abuse, reluctance to have children, and employment instability. After a trip together to Europe (in which he resented having to visit her in the hospital after she re-injured her back), she separated from him when they returned to the USA.

Eileen was an orphan and probably impressed by the young poet she met back in 1941. Although her life with John revealed his flaws clearly and must have entailed much suffering for her, she was able to build up a career for herself and develop the self-confidence to leave him to his own self-destructive path.

He then met Ann Levine, a young woman in her early twenties, soon after he arrived at Minnesota, and married her in 1956. They had a son Paul in 1957, toward whom John felt much affection and much resentment. By 1958, Ann had become disenchanted with John, and she left him in 1959.

In 1961, he met and married Kate Donahue, also in her early twenties, whose mother had died when she was young and whose father had been an alcoholic, the ideal wife for an aging alcoholic. They remained married until John's suicide. A daughter was born in 1962 and another in 1971. Kate eventually began to study to be a teacher, pursuing a career like Eileen before her.

His Social Presence

The frequent moves in his career led to John being lonely a lot. For example, when he first arrived in England in 1936 he knew no one and craved for company. This led him to behave inappropriately when he was in company. He would become over-excited to the point of dominating the conversation and insulting people. An acquaintance in England described his moods as hysterical joy, deep depression and obvious boredom. His social style was affected by his nervousness and self-doubts, to which John reacted by being noisy, boastful and bullying. His drinking exacerbated this public persona.

At his first teaching position at Wayne State University, he drank black coffee and chain-smoked. He was thin and had a bushy mustache. He bathed infrequently and wore such dirty clothes that he stank. John's biographer sums up John's style at Princeton between 1943 and 1953 as a braggart, womanizer, drinker and formidable intellectual. John was also consumed by insecurity over his worth as a poet and self-recriminations over his adulteries. He felt hateful, unworthy, pitiable, and could be paranoid about his critics. John admitted that sex and alcohol became the props for his existence.

His Psychiatric State

John experienced depression quite frequently. It could be brought on by loneliness, doubts about his adequacy as a writer, breakups with his women, and by his physical exhaustion. His first 'breakdown' seems to have occurred while in New York after his return from England when he was having great difficulty finding a job, his writings were being rejected, and his fiancé Beatrice was in England.

During his first semester at Wayne State University, the stress he created for himself by his work habits, loneliness, social ineptitude, and separation from Beatrice, all eventually led to a breakdown. He was exhausted at times, sullen and angry at others, and eventually began talking of demons and passing out. Soon after the beginning of the second semester, John collapsed and was examined by psychiatrists. One diagnosed post-epileptic confusion; another psychoneurotic maladjustment and possible schizophrenia. With the help of his friends, John hung on and finished the semester. John eventually came to believe that he suffered from *petit mal* epilepsy and took medication for it for much of his life.

Thereafter his state gradually grew worse. During a period of unemployment in 1943, while married to Eileen, John was exhausted, undernourished, sleeping badly, suffering from indigestion, and his scalp was burning and itching. He feared another attack of *petit mal*. He thought of suicide and wrote that only his relationship with Eileen prevented him. His biographer labels these symptoms as psychosomatic and hysterical.

In 1947, after John's love affair with Lise ended, John saw a psychiatrist for a few years (until 1953). His diaries list many of the symptoms he presented to his psychiatrist over the years and which he analyzed in detail - little habits such as his aversion to opening mail or answering the door or the telephone, his emotional numbness, his eczema and fear of baldness, his pleasure in pimples and blackheads, his hatred of women, and the problems with his father and mother. (At one point, he worried whether his sexual excesses were rooted in homosexual tendencies.) John was an intellectual, and he wrote poems about his suffering. He seems to have become obsessed by his symptoms, and his self-absorption made them far worse. He analyzed his dreams in his diaries and tried to make sense of his mind. John worried about things that do not merit worry, and then he worried about his worrying.

This is perhaps a problem with all psychologically-oriented intellectuals, and those who keep diaries permit us to monitor their self-absorption. Many grow out of this, eventually reaching a measure of peace in old age. However, John's preoccupation with himself-as-a-problem grew during his life.

In 1954, John was hired by the University of Iowa. He fell soon after his arrival, breaking his wrist and damaging his ankles. He suffered from colitis, was lonely, sexually deprived, and not eating well. He slept very little, drank a lot and had hallucinations. He got into a fight with his landlord one night and was put in jail. The University dismissed him.

John arrived in Minnesota in 1954. There his health deteriorated and his drinking increased steadily. After his second divorce, he was frequently hospitalized for brief periods. Eventually he was diagnosed as an alcoholic and after his third marriage was treated on several occasions for alcoholism. He entered treatment for alcoholism in 1966 and 1967, but not seriously until late 1969. He was diagnosed as an alcohol and drug abuser. A list of drugs used revealed: sleeping pills since 1949, nerve pills since 1955, phenobarbital since 1959, Haldol, Vivactic and Tuinol since May 1969, Serax since November 1969, Thorazine since May 1969, Nembutal in 1961, and Librium occasionally. He also smoked five packs of cigarettes a day.

He had great trouble staying off alcohol and had to be re-admitted several times. He joined Alcoholics Anonymous and worked hard at fighting the craving. In 1970, one doctor diagnosed him as having a cyclothymic personality (with swings from depression to elation). Another felt that John was not psychotic when sober, but that he had a fear of insanity and of committing suicide.

John's Suicide

In 1971, John was still married to Kate, but Kate was now a school teacher. The marriage had severe problems. They had tried marriage therapy (back in 1969). Their sexual relationship was poor. They had one daughter and Kate was pregnant with another child. (Sarah was born in June, 1971). In June, John moved his mother from New York to an apartment opposite his house in Minneapolis. John, who needed his wife's full attention, was facing the coming of another baby in the house, and his mother drove him crazy with her demands. Kate was tired of the constant demands he made on her and was tired of his alcoholism. It would not have been surprising if John had feared that Kate would leave him soon.

John's income was higher now than ever before. In 1971, his total income reached thirty-one thousand dollars. After years of financial insecurity, he was better off. But he might have been afraid of the effects of his alcoholism on his future income, especially if his writing suffered. (He had defaulted on his child support payments in 1962 and 1966, and Ann had to take him to court.)

John's confidence in his ability to write well had gone. He was beginning to recognize that he no longer had the perseverance to finish any major work. He also began to lose confidence in his teaching ability. Although many of his students remember his teaching as outstanding, one commentator noted that John preferred to teach undergraduates (who would be more likely to worship him) which suggests an underlying self-doubt about his ability as a teacher. He had reverted to Catholicism, and his biographer believes that John retained his faith in God.

John began to drink again, although there was no alcohol in his blood after his death. On Wednesday January 5th, 1972, he left the house intending to kill himself. His note read "I am a nuisance." He came home. On Friday January 7th he left again, telling Kate "You won't have to worry about me any more." He took the bus to the University and walked to the Washington Avenue Bridge. At about nine in the morning, he climbed over the railings and jumped without looking back. He fell one hundred feet, landing near the pier of the municipal coal docks, rolling fifteen feet or so down the embankment.

Discussion

In some ways, this is the simple story of the slow disintegration of an alcoholic. John, beginning life with some psychological problems, gradually turns more and more to alcohol as a solution, and eventually killed himself as do many alcoholics.

However, the fact that John's father, who was portrayed to him by his mother as a spiritless, sexless, effete wastrel, committed suicide clearly must have been a critical event in John's development. It is noteworthy that early on, at South Kent School, John used an attempt at suicide as a solution to the problem of being bullied. Despite the negative view John developed of his father, he probably identified with his father as a child, and the suicide of his role model would lead him to see suicide as an attractive alternative in crisis situations.

The death of his school mate and later, when he was at Harvard University, of his good friend Bhain Campbell from cancer would have been more traumatic because of the earlier death of his father. The experience of one loss often sensitizes a person to subsequent losses.

His father's suicide served to make John more dependent on his overpossessive mother, who was not very affectionate despite her love for her children. His relationship with his mother must have hindered his relationships with other women. Sometimes he put his mother's concerns before those of his lovers and wives. He also must have feared that women would try to possess him in the way that his mother had tried to.

It is also noteworthy that his personal style was so unpleasant that it must have alienated others from him, increasing his fears that he was not worthy. No wonder that he strove for sexual conquests, for they would prop up his insecure sense of self-worth. He preferred to teach undergraduates who would be more likely to like him as a teacher. He married young women, often lacking self-confidence in themselves, two of whom eventually found the confidence to free themselves from bondage to him.

John suffered from tremendous insecurity about his self-worth. The weak and sickly kid at school developed into an abrasive self-absorbed adult. Was he any good as a teacher, as a poet, as a son, husband or father, or as a lover? Despite the successes of his life (teaching jobs at good universities, acclaim for his poems, and three marriages), he continued to be plagued by doubts, and to alienate those who wanted to be close to him. At the age of fifty-seven, rather than reaping the rewards from his earlier successes, he seemed to be facing failure. His poetry was perhaps no longer good. His craving for alcohol was as hard to fight as ever, and his marriage was disintegrating. Sexual liaisons would probably become rare.

He could have continued the struggle and sought to improve himself. But his past attempts had not proved successful. Perhaps he had lost hope that future efforts would succeed? Rather than face a continuing decline, John chose the solution that his father had chosen forty-five years earlier.

Hart Crane[2]

Hart Crane was born on July 21, 1899, in Garrettsville, Ohio, as Harold Hart Crane. (He adopted his mother's surname as his first name when he was eighteen and sided with his mother during his parents' divorce.) His father's family could trace their ancestors back to English ancestors who arrived in 1646. His grandfather ran the biggest store in Garrettsville, was a director of the local bank, and ran a maple-syrup cannery. His mother's family, the Harts, traced their line back to New England settlers and were also in business.

His mother, Grace Hart, had visited Garrettsville and met his father, Clarence (C.A.) Crane in 1898. After a brief romance, they married, on June 1, 1898. The marriage was a failure from the beginning. Grace was terrified by sex. As a result, Clarence found her cold, and she found him lustful. Hart was torn by their conflict and this, more than any other factor, accounts for his life style and his eventual suicide. Hart initially took his mother's side, but toward the end of his brief life he took his father's side. To an outside observer, however, Grace is clearly at fault. Her terror of sex alienated her husband and caused her to turn to her son as her fantasied lover. She became obsessed with Hart, devoting herself after his suicide to building up his reputation and trying (unsuccessfully) to obliterate the record of her pathological behavior. She even tried to communicate with Hart through mediums. Hart's homosexuality was partly the result of Grace's pathology. Hart killed himself at the age of thirty-three, jumping from a boat bringing him from Mexico to New York City.

Hart's Childhood

Hart was not sickly but was considered delicate. His relatives waited for the first signs of the allergies that ran in the Crane family, but Hart had none at first. They would develop later. Hart was precocious, walking, talking and reading at an early age.

By age three he showed feminine interests. He liked to play with his aunt's dress-making materials and to decorate hats. His aunt and mother were concerned by this and forbad such play. When Hart was five, the family moved to Warren, Ohio, where Hart led a more typical kid's life.

---

[2] This section is based on Unterecker (1969).

The business ventures of his father and the marital conflict between his parents consumed his parents' energy. Hart learned that he could get their attention and approval by being witty and clever and by being sick. If he was criticized by his parents, Hart would fall ill with what we would now call psychosomatic complaints. He had fits in which he would vomit and cry hysterically. Both Hart and his mother came to believe that his illnesses were a direct result of her unkindness or insensitivity.

In 1908, the marital conflict became so severe that Grace entered a private sanitorium and C.A. moved to Chicago. Hart, age nine, was sent to live with his grandparents in Cleveland. There he had an indulgent grandmother, servants and much freedom. In 1909, both of his parents moved in with Hart's grandparents.

By age eleven, Hart was interested in the theater, painted, took piano lessons, and loved to write. He read rather than play outdoors. It was then that he told his grandmother that he wanted to be a poet. His teenage years seem relatively uneventful. He tried smoking, both cigars and a pipe. He was caught playing with a neighbor's daughter. And he had his first homosexual experience with a young man who worked for the family.

His biographer is reticent about Hart's homosexuality. He minimizes it, fails to describe Hart's lovers and the path of his affairs, and generally treats it as if it were not important. The fact is that Hart, as already noted, had the kind of mother who moves a son (particularly an only child) toward homosexuality. He had an early seduction about which we are told nothing. And he spent his adult life cruising waterfront bars picking up sailors for quick sex. Hart spoke of love, but none of his sailors stayed for long, a few months at the most. He never managed to establish a long-term homosexual relationship. In the early 1900s, homosexual encounters were probably uncommon, especially in the midwest. Hart, even with an inclination (conscious or unconscious) to develop into a homosexual, might never have encountered the opportunity, ending up a latent homosexual. In this context, an early homosexual encounter looms as critical.

At this time too, though he occasionally dated, Hart was telling his mother that she was more beautiful than girls his own age and was his real sweetheart. He felt that she was in need of his protection more than "common girls." It is likely that Grace encouraged this unhealthy attachment.

In January 1913, his grandfather died. Hart had not been as close to his grandfather as to his grandmother, but it was an upsetting experience to watch his grandfather fall sick and die. His grandfather left Hart a legacy of $5,000 to be given to him once his grandmother died.

Hart entered a good high school in January, 1914, and he attended intermittently for the next three years. He was not active in school. He joined no clubs, played no sports, and did not write for the school newspaper or magazine. He was in the college-oriented program, but he was frequently absent. For example, he took one semester off to go with his mother and grandmother to visit their house in an island off Cuba.

Hart had built up a good library in his room at his grandmother's. When he wrote poetry, he would smoke cigars or smell his mother's perfume (or other odors such as the maid's sweaty shoes) in order to get himself into a poetic mood. His first poem appeared in print in the Greenwich Village Bruno's Weekly in September, 1916.

Hart also showed moodiness, moving from high elation to deep depression. At his grandmother's Caribbean island house in late 1914, his parents had a very bad argument, and C.A. left for the USA. Grace turned to Hart as a confidante, not noticing how depressed he was becoming. In early 1915, Hart made two suicide attempts, one by slashing his wrists and another by swallowing his mother's Veronal powders. It is clear that his parents' violent quarrels and their "violent sexual reconciliations" (as he described them to friends) left him very upset, to the point of physical illness. On the other hand, when his parents were away, he was lonely.

In 1916, Hart was a "published" poet but unhappy at school, so he decided to quit school. In November, after a particularly bad row, C.A. moved out, and Hart's parents filed for divorce. Hart had a second poem published (in The Pagan), and so it was agreed that he could quit school, ostensibly to find a job to help support his mother. In this confused time, Hart's parents decided that he could go and live in New York City, thinking that he would study for the entrance exams for Columbia University. Hart made only token efforts in this direction, but started instead on the life path that would lead to his decline and suicide.

Hart's life makes sense in the light of his psychological disturbance, and so it makes sense to briefly review his problems.

Depression

Hart suffered continually from depression. This could be brought on by letters from his mother or his father when they tried to involve him in their affairs, his poverty, his loneliness or the rejection of his poems. His biographer mentions periods of elation, and so this raises the possibility of a bipolar affective disorder. However, there is not sufficient information in the biography to make such a diagnosis, and Unterecker gives no information about the presence of psychiatric disorder in Hart's relatives. His maternal grandparents seemed to have been free from any disorder.

Hart suffered from insomnia for most of his life and, in addition, he suffered at times from nightmares so that he preferred insomnia to sleep.

Alcoholism

Initially, Hart drank to overcome his shyness in company and for poetic inspiration. He would begin a composition when drunk and polish it later. However, his drinking quickly grew out of control until he was drinking up to nine scotches at a time (by his own admission in 1927) or a half a gallon of bootleg wine in 1928. By his late-twenties, Hart was clearly an alcoholic, suffering from delirium tremens. In 1927, Yvor Winters described Hart:

> .....he regarded Crane as a man of "more or less manic-depressive make-up" and.....was shocked to find that "his hair was graying, his skin had the dull red color with reticulated grayish traceries which so often go with advanced alcoholism, and his ears and knuckles were beginning to look like those of a pugilist. (Unterecker, 1969, p. 526)

Hart was only 28 at the time! (His hair was white by the next year.)

Hart would go on drinking sprees for days at a time, often being picked up dead drunk by friends, sometimes getting into fights and being arrested by the police (in New York City in 1927, Paris in 1929 and Mexico in 1931).

Paranoia

Hart seems to have had paranoid tendencies toward the end of his life. He felt betrayed by his friends and parents and, when he was drunk, he would list his grievances against them. He often got into fights with taxi drivers whom he felt had overcharged him.

Hart typically blamed others for his misfortunes, never apparently realising what an unpleasant person he was. He borrowed money from friends, moved in with them, interrupted them whenever he needed company, destroyed their property, and insulted them. He behaved like a pampered brat, immature, with the self-centeredness of a child. Friends eventually asked him to leave, though he would often storm out before he pushed them to the brink.

By 1928, Hart was becoming increasingly violent when drunk, and his landladies and friends frequently hid from him in fear during what were described as his "incoherent attacks." His behavior deteriorated still further during his final year in Mexico.

His paranoia was, therefore, based in part on real events, but they were events he brought on himself.

Physical Illnesses

Hart suffered a lot from psychosomatic illnesses - hay fever and hives in particular. He also from time to time had boils, back ache, and occasional tonsillitis, urethritis (which he thought at first was venereal disease) and conjunctivitis. His eyesight was also poor. However, Unterecker suggests that Hart enjoyed his illnesses, and they certainly elicited sympathy from his friends.

Suicide Attempts

His first documented suicide attempts were in 1915 when on vacation with his mother after his father had stormed back to Cleveland. He slashed his wrists and took an overdose. Unterecker does not mention suicidal behavior again until Hart's final year of life spent in Mexico.

Interestingly, his friend Harry Crosby shot himself in December, 1929, in New York, and Hart was with Harry's wife and mother that evening and helped them cope with the shocking event.

Homosexuality

Initially, in Akron in 1919, in Cleveland in 1921 to 1923 and in New York City in 1924, Hart fell in love with and had, albeit brief, affairs with men. But Hart's homosexuality soon developed into a pattern in which he would cruise parks in Cleveland or waterfront bars in New York City and elsewhere looking for casual sex. Occasionally, these casual episodes developed into relationships that lasted weeks or months, but this was not typical. In many of these episodes, Hart was drunk, and it was not uncommon for Hart to be beaten up and robbed during his visits to the waterfront. In 1922 he was blackmailed after a casual encounter. When he was in Washington, DC, in 1920 working for his father, and in California for six months with his mother in 1927 and 1928, he became involved with groups of homosexual friends, and he went to orgiastic parties. But Hart failed to find a stable lover.

It must remembered that homosexuality was not so accepted or open in the 1920s as now and that Hart was from the conservative midwest. He never really felt comfortable about his homosexuality. He may have assuaged his guilt by making sex a brutal experience and by getting beaten up by truckers or sailors who objected to his advances. He was typically drunk during his sexual searches, probably to overcome his guilt. When he finally fell in love with a woman for the first time, Peggy Cowley in Mexico in 1931, he seemed overjoyed to be normal for the first time, though very quickly he had to supplement intercourse with Peggy by casual homosexual encounters with Mexican boys.

Hart and His Parents

His emotional life was dominated by his parents. At first, there were daily letters back and forth and an intimate involvement with the details of one another's lives, especially between Grace and Hart. After his parents' divorce, he sided with his mother and became alienated from his father. In time, he became more and more aware of the suffocating possessiveness of his mother. In 1928 he fled from her home in California and spent the rest of his life hiding his whereabouts from her. Upon breaking with his mother, he became close to his father.

Hart's mother had continual breakdowns, and her letters to Hart would plunge him into anxiety or depression and interfere with his writing. When he stayed with his mother he fought with her, and yet he was lonely without her. Eventually her jealousy over his relationship with his father, his friends and his homosexual lovers (after he had confessed to her) drove him away. Hart's mother was the neurotic mother often found in background of disturbed sons. Hart eventually fled from her, but far too late in his life to achieve independence and maturity.

Hart's father seems to have been a normal, pleasant, conservative businessman. Despite the odd life style of his son, he was willing to support his efforts to be a good poet, and he sent him money regularly once Hart reconciled with him.

Hart and His Friends

Hart made many friends and had hundreds of acquaintances. His friends lent him money to live on, let him stay with them, critiqued his work, and went to plays, restaurants and bars with him. He carried on a voluminous correspondence with them and they with him.

Yet a frequent cry of Hart's was that he was so lonely. Of course, he alienated his friends by his drunken and abusive behavior but, amazingly, many remained tolerant of him. His loneliness suggests a couple of possibilities. First, that these "friendships" were not close, close enough to form the social bonds that people need. Or second, that they could not replace the need we all have for a primary tie, usually with a lover or spouse. Hart kept his overly close ties to his parents long after others have moved on, maintained a large circle of "friends", and looked for orgasms in toilets and dark alleyways. None of these can replace deep and meaningful relationships.

Hart's Efforts To Support Himself

Hart's adult life consisted of a series of moves from one city to another and long periods of half-hearted job-hunting interspersed with brief periods of work. He lived in rented rooms, other people's apartments and houses, or with his mother or father. The list of his travels is long: New York, Cleveland, New York, Cleveland, Akron, Washington DC, Cleveland, New York, Woodstock, New York, Pawling NY, New York, Isle of Pines, New York, Patterson NY, Los Angeles, Patterson, New York, France, New York, and thence to Mexico. His moves were made on the basis of lovers he had, friends offering to support him, searches for jobs, and retreats back to his parents.

His attempts to get work fit a classic pattern: an individual who develops a perception of himself as a writer and resents the effort needed to develop a secure career. Hart worked - as a temporary salesman in bookstores, as a low level copy-writer in advertising agencies, and for his father in his father's stores. But he spent most of his time "searching" for jobs. He lived off loans from friends (which he did repay) and toward the end of his life on monthly checks from his father. In 1925 Otto Kahn gave him $2000 (and an additional $500 in 1927) to write poetry. In 1929, his grandmother died, and he received his inheritance of $5000 which he spent in eight months on a trip to France followed by a stay in New York City. In 1931, he received a Guggenheim fellowship for $2000 and went to Mexico for a year.

When he received these large sums of money, he spent them quickly and foolishly. He gave no serious thought to establishing a stable base, though he had fantasies of stable work in an advertising agency and of owning a house in the country. His income from writing was miniscule, and his attempts to write stories, plays, movie scripts and magazine articles came to nothing, more through his lack of persistence than from rejections from editors and publishers.

His adult life, therefore, was dominated by his poverty. Like a pampered child, he blamed others for his failures. He seemed not to acknowledge the role of his alcoholism, his laziness, his failure to go to college, or his general lack of motivation and persistence. He seemed to think that his parents had a duty to support him throughout his life and that he could remain a dependent child.

Yet, at the same time, he also realized his failure, especially in contrast to his father, a successful businessman. When it came down to a final reckoning, Hart knew that he had failed in his career, in his friendships, in his love life, and probably as a writer. By age thirty-three his life was over, and he could look forward only to the life of a derelict.

Hart's Poetry

Hart had some success as a poet. After publishing occasional poems in small magazines, he sold his first poem (for ten dollars) in 1919. His first collection (White Buildings) was published in 1926, after two years of sending the manuscript around to publishing houses, and it received an enthusiastic reception, along with some criticisms. Hart was pleased with its reception. He worked for years on a long poem, eventually published as The Bridge in 1930 to more negative and critical reviews, though Hart was awarded the Levinson Prize by Poetry that year.

However, by 1928 Hart was finding it hard to write. As his reputation grew, magazines began to solicit work from him, but he had nothing to send. After The Bridge, Hart wrote very little. He tried writing articles for Fortune and book reviews, but finished only a couple of pieces. His alcoholism and deteriorating social relationships did not make writing easier. In 1930, Howard Lovecraft wrote of Hart:

> Poor devil - he has "arrived" at last as a standard
> American poet seriously regarded by all reviewers &
> critics; yet at the very crest of his fame he is on
> the verge of psychological, physical, & financial
> disintegration, & with no certainty of ever having the
> inspiration to write a major work of literature again.
> (Unterecker, 1969, p. 626)

The Final Year

Hart's final year of life was spent in Mexico as a Guggenheim fellow. It was a failure. Rather than writing, Hart continued to deteriorate. He stayed almost permanently drunk, sought homosexual pick-ups, and abused and insulted friends and acquaintances there.

He wrote a couple of poems, one book review and an article. But his plans for a play, an epic poem, a series of book reviews and a series of articles were abandoned. His fear that he was finished as a writer grew.

> ....he seemed full of doubts about what he had
> written and full of doubts about whether he could
> ever write anything more. He seemed very depressed
> and in a sort of hopeless state of mind.....
> (Unterecker, 1969, p. 683)

Then, soon after his arrival there, his father died, and Hart went back to Cleveland for the funeral. (His grandmother had died in September 1928.) This must have been a severe loss for him since he had grown close to his father in recent years now that he was completely alienated from his mother. One result of his father's death was an expectation of being able to live on his inheritance, but soon problems arose with how much this would be and how regular the checks would come.

In December, 1931, he fell in love with Peggy Cowley who had come to Mexico to divorce Malcolm Cowley. He was overjoyed at having fallen in love with a woman at last, but he was soon soliciting Mexican boys. Peggy moved in with him, and they began to quarrel continually. His intake of alcohol increased, and he worried about his inheritance and his literary reputation. He was particularly worried about how his latest poem would be reviewed.

> Moroseness and anger against the world possessed him.....He became an ugly, sick man in mind and body. Constant tirades against the servants, Mexico, his friends in the States.....Mexico was destroying him. His friends despised his work. The world despised his work. He was a failure as a poet, the laughing stock of his friends.
> (Unterecker, 1969, pp. 737, 751)

One day in April, he decided to kill himself. With Peggy and a friend helping him, he tried to draft a will. Then he took some iodine and later some mercurochrome, after which his stomach was pumped. Peggy persuaded him that he had to go back to America, though he was afraid to return there. They left by boat on April 23rd, 1932.

During a stop in Havana, Hart went off for a homosexual encounter but became angry at Peggy. What had she done in Havana? Why hadn't she returned to the boat? (She had been waiting for him in a restaurant!) He became drunk and violent. A night watchman on the boat prevented him jumping overboard, but Hart jumped successfully to his death around noon the next day, on April 27th.

Discussion

Hart Crane was many things. He was an alcoholic and a violent and abusive person, with little regard for others. He was a pampered child, spoilt by his parents and grandparents, and he decided that living off them was an acceptable life style. Though his alienation from his relatives and their deaths pained him a great deal, there was always their inheritances for him to squander as he continued his downward path.

But he was also a poet and might have been a productive poet if his life circumstances had been otherwise. He had little to support his self-esteem. After all, he failed to develop a career or to form a stable life (with home and lover). All he had was his poetry.

Literary matters consumed him, both the esthetics and the politics. This made him vulnerable, for he became involved in the politics of the literary world and its squabbles. The reception of his poetry was critical to his feelings of self-worth. Some of his work was praised, but much was not. Even successful writers must face rejection after rejection at times. And Hart's experience was no different. His first collection of poems was passed from publisher to publisher for almost two years before getting accepted. Then, when he was receiving recognition, his creative powers declined. Perhaps they would have declined anyway, but his increasing alcohol abuse and unstable life may have been sufficient cause in themselves.

It is always interesting to ask what would have happened had the person not killed himself. What would Hart Crane have become? A drunken bum in New York City? Perhaps robbed, beaten up and killed by the sailors one day at the waterfront? An isolate for sure, for he was rapidly becoming so abusive that his friends and acquaintances would soon have abandoned him. And yet what might have happened if his father had not died and if Hart had gone to live with him? His times there seemed to have been the happiest and quietest periods of his life and as close to normal as Hart ever came. But, probably, Hart's lack of self-control would have driven him from Ohio, back to New York and to the path of chronic self-destruction that he had chosen for himself.

Mark Gertler[3]

Louis and Golda Gertler came from Przemysl, Galicia, a border country on a tributary of the Vistula between Russia, Austria and Poland about sixty miles west of Lvov. They emigrated to London in 1890, but poverty forced them to return after a few months. During their brief stay in London, a son Max was born, the youngest of the five children by seven years.

Back in Przemysl, his relatives bought Louis an inn to run but, through bad luck or bad management, the inn did not prosper. After its failure, Louis tried to sell boots and then buttons but failed again. In despair he left to go to America, promising to send for his family later. They lived in poverty supported by meager wages from the oldest son, Harry, and food brought home by Golda from the Jewish restaurant where she worked. The children stole food for the family, and they suffered persecution both from being Jewish and from being poor.

After five years, Louis asked his family to meet him in London, and so in 1896 Golda Gertler emigrated for the second time. The family

---

[3] This section is based on Woodeson (1972).

stayed temporarily in one room in the apartment of a friend in Shoreditch. Max, later called Mark, recalled waking up that first night and experiencing his first real fit of depression.

Early Days

This time Louis got work, at first only smoothing walking-sticks, but gradually the family established itself, staying for three years in one room and eventually moving to better and better rooms and earning a little more money. Mark was sent to the local Jewish school, but the local authorities forced his parents to send him to the public school. Mark acquired his name on the first day of school when the registration official could not understand Golda's pronunciation of Max and wrote down the name as Mark.

Mark described himself as a nervous, high strung and emotional boy, somewhat undersized, thin and pale, always tired since he never got to bed until the family retired at midnight or later. At school, he was quiet, conscientious and well-liked. He liked drawing, and Golda encouraged him in this. He would become so engrossed in his drawing that he ignored meals and drew for hours, oblivious to his surroundings. The family was religious, and Mark had his *barmitzvah* in 1904.

When Mark left school in January, 1906, he knew he wanted to be a painter. This perplexed his parents who did not view it as an appropriate career, but they decided to give him a chance. A family friend took him along to the Regent Street Polytechnic and persuaded them to let him enroll. Mark worked hard for two years there. In the summer of 1907 he did well in the examinations, except for failing design. However, his family found the fees too high, and so Mark took a job at a neighboring firm of glass painters, working days and going to classes at nights. In the summer of 1908, he again did well in the examinations, except for failing design. In the National Art Competition, with fifteen thousand competitors, he won a bronze medal.

At this point the Jewish Educational Aid Society agreed to pay his tuition, and they referred him to the painter William Rothstein. Rothstein liked what he saw and helped Mark gain admission to the Slade School of Art. He began there on October 13, 1908.

Apprenticeship

Mark's life was centered on art. He remained diffident toward women and only slowly adjusted to being around gentiles. However, during his second term, he became friendly with C. R. W. Nevinson who brought him into closer contact with the other students. At the end of the first year at the Slade, Mark was awarded one of the two scholarships.

Friendship with Nevinson opened doors for Mark. Nevinson's parents liked him and introduced him to their friends and to the ways of the middle-class. He joined a small exhibiting group, the Friday Club, had his work reviewed in the newspapers, and met intellectuals.

In September 1911, one his friends, Maxwell Lightfoot, a student at the Slade and five years older than Mark, fell in love with an artist's model of whom his parents disapproved. Lightfoot decided to go ahead and marry her anyway but before the wedding found out that she was notoriously promiscuous. He cut his throat on the day before the wedding.

Mark remained close to his family. He painted at home, and his mother was one of his favorite subjects. Mark remained close to his brothers, and they helped him financially later in life. His first love affair was with May Berlinski who lived just two doors away, but his first sexual experience was with a prostitute paid for by his brothers.

In 1911, Mark's painting of his mother was shown in the New English Art Club and was bought by a discerning collector, he was awarded a British Institute scholarship, and he was elected to membership in two prestigious art societies. Such success for a young artist was almost unheard of in England.

In April, 1912, Mark moved in with his brother Harry and his wife. They gave him the top floor and, though he liked his studio, the noise of the children and the family bothered him. In 1912 he became friendly with Dora Carrington, a fellow student at the Slade, and was soon in love with her. The affair with Dora brought Mark great pain. Since Nevinson was also attracted to her, Mark's love for Dora destroyed his friendship with Nevinson. But more than that, Dora was a sexually inhibited and emotionally unstable woman. Her relationship with Mark lasted until 1917 when she fell in love with and moved in with Lytton Strachey.

Mark and Dora had many good times together, and there was a sympathy and understanding between them. They explored London together, helped each other's painting, and wrote to each other almost daily. But Mark's desire to sleep with Dora and to marry her led to continual squabbling between them. Dora did not agree to be Mark's lover until she had already met and fallen in love with Lytton Strachey, and Mark always knew that she did not enjoy sex with him. All too often, Mark blamed himself for the difficulties with Dora, viewing himself as vulgar and disagreeable.

Life As A Painter

Early in his career, Mark began to have occasional problems finding inspiration for his painting. In 1919 he wrote to friends that he was finding art absolutely beyond him. It was unfortunate for Mark, along with other British painters, that the Parisian artists were taking the art world by storm with post-Impressionism, Fauvism, and Cubism. Mark was aware he had mastered techniques which suddenly looked out-of-date. Mark was confronted by a dilemma. Should he continue to develop his style, yet run the risk of not being seen as good as the Parisians, or should he modify his style toward the Parisian styles? Mark chose the former path, and today we have all heard of Picasso while few have heard of Gertler.

Yet his art was the major focus of his life. Outside of his art, there was nothing, he felt, to hope for. During these early years, he began to suffer from the headaches that plagued him throughout his life, and he continued to experience depressions. To a large extent, his mother's love and her need for him kept him from suicide during these severe depressions.

By 1912, Mark had made another close friend, a fellow painter, John Currie. They exhibited their work together and received equally favorable reviews in the papers. Currie introduced Mark to Edward Marsh, a member of the upper classes who was secretary to Neville Chamberlain and later Winston Churchill. Marsh bought Mark's paintings and later contributed a regular stipend to support him.

Mark's entries first into the middle classes and then to the upper classes were extraordinary experiences for him. Before visiting friends of Marsh for a weekend, Golda had to rush and buy Mark the first pair of pajamas he had ever owned. Yet Mark was able quickly to fit into these new social strata, and he remained unashamed about his roots. He was happy to take his new friends to Yiddish plays, the Jewish sections of London, and to his own home for tea.

By 1913, Mark was finding it hard to survive. He found it hard to paint portraits for the conventional market, and his work was not of the kind that bought success in the leading London art circles. His brothers contributed a little, and Marsh bought some paintings. He moved from depression to elation, but his paintings of 1913 were not received well. In desperation, Mark applied for a part-time position teaching art at the Boys Foundation School in Whitechapel but was rejected. One of his friends, the writer Gilbert Cannan, introduced Mark to Lady Ottoline Morrell, and she liked his work and decided to get Mark's career launched. She showed his work at one of her evening salons, and introduced him to many of the leading painters. Although Mark did become more well known as a result of her efforts, the war in 1914 seriously inhibited art sales.

In 1914, John Currie murdered his lover and killed himself. Thereafter, no new friendships with fellow artists developed, and Mark faced the problems in his work alone. Mark decided around this time to find his own place in London, and he rented a small apartment in Hampstead. For the first year, the stipend from Marsh paid his living expenses. 1914 ended on a positive note. He had an affair with a former Slade student, Iris Tree, his reputation was on the rise again, he was invited to join one of the groups which had rejected him earlier, and doctors assured him that he was physically healthy.

Independence

Although Mark no longer had an artist as an intimate friend, he had many friends, including D. H. Lawrence, Katherine Mansfield, and a good friend S. S. Koteliansky (Kot). The war brought fears of deportation for his parents, and service in the military for Mark. [4] His parents were spared when they found a way to be declared Polish. Mark's opposition to the war also brought a crisis of conscience over his friendship with Marsh, and in late 1915 he gave up the stipend from Marsh.

He struggled through 1916, with little income and endless heartache from his relationship with Dora Carrington. His headaches continued to be severe. But once more Mark was saved by a patron, Monty Shearman. In 1916 Mark tried sculpture and writing poetry and plays but, by the end of the year, he had given up these avenues.

In February 1917, Mark's father died at the age of sixty. Mark's relationship with Carrington continued to cause him pain, and hardly anyone would buy his paintings. The spells of depression grew worse. His friend Gilbert Cannan, a writer, became insane and was hospitalized. Mark struggled on, but there were signs of an imminent breakdown. In 1918, Mark ran into Carrington and Strachey in London and physically attacked Strachey. Mark and Kot also vandalized Monty Shearman's apartment. When Carrington married in 1921, Mark went out to buy a gun with which to kill himself, but all the shops were closed. Mark sought release in drink, parties and sex. Mark's close friendships with Lady Ottoline, Monty Shearman and Kot helped him through this period.

After the war, at the same time as Mark's paintings began to attract more positive attention, his physical health worsened. He was offered his first one-man show in London for March 1921, and he worked hard. But in November 1920 he collapsed with tuberculosis and was sent to a sanitorium in Scotland.

The Routine

Mark was released from the sanitorium in May 1921, and he drastically changed his life. From now on he set up a routine which he followed almost rigidly. He restricted his social activities to a few evenings a week. Callers were barred except on Thursday evenings. He worked diligently for the same hours each day - 10.30 am to 12.30 pm and 2 pm to 4.30 pm. He walked each morning on Hampstead Heath. His landlady provided him with meals. Despite this care, he still suffered from severe migraine headaches and had several relapses which sent him back to the sanitorium (in 1925, 1929, and 1936). Though

---

[4] Interestingly, many years before, Mark's father had used self-inflicted wounds to get out of military service.

tuberculosis killed Katherine Mansfield and D. H. Lawrence, Mark's seemed to been cured, and his breakdowns were mainly nervous in origin. He often went to his brothers for the Friday sabbath, he visited Lady Ottoline's country estate, and he had several affairs, many of them with models. He travelled a little, usually with a rich friend, Walter Taylor. His work sold well enough to provide a reasonable income. One gallery gave him an advance of three hundred pounds a year against sales, and from 1921 to 1932 he had no pressing financial worries. Indeed, for much of the 1920s, Mark was almost happy.

He continued to agonize about his art, however. He would be filled with doubts about his value as an artist. He saw himself as inferior to Matisse or Picasso, and sometimes the torment would drive him to consider suicide. In November 1929 he again went out to buy a revolver, but did not do so.

In the mid 1920s, Mark met Majorie Hodgkinson, another former Slade student, about ten years his junior. They become good friends and, when Mark went to a sanitorium in 1929, she accompanied him and stayed nearby. In April 1930, while they were visiting Paris, they were married by the British Consul. Majorie was not Jewish, but his mother soon accepted the marriage.

In 1930, Mark's brothers went into bankruptcy, and he realized that he could no longer rely on them to help him financially. Golda died in February 1932 from pneumonia. Lytton Strachey died the same month, and Carrington shot herself in March. Majorie thus became much more important to Mark. Majorie was ill a lot, and often both she and Mark would be sick, and they would have to get a nurse. They had a son in August 1932 but, the next time Majorie became pregnant, they arranged an abortion.

Mark's life now was in constant flux. The owner of the gallery which bought his works died. He and Marjorie moved several times. And there was a baby in his life, disturbing his peace. The child needed several operations, and the cost of these led to financial strain. In 1936, Mark's headaches and depression grew so severe that he went into a sanitorium again. Marjorie went with him, but they decided to separate for at least three months. Mark slashed his wrists while there, but called the nurse in time to be saved.

Mark left the sanitorium in October 1936, and he and Marjorie moved into a new house, bought with a mortgage raised by her father. Mark found a new gallery to take his paintings. In 1937, their nurse left, and they decided to cope with their son alone. Mark took up teaching to ease the overdraft at the bank, but his migraine headaches became more frequent, and his depressions continued.

Mark decided that painting was the most important aspect of his life, more important to him than his family. Marjorie who had withdrawn from him sexually and who already had been attracted to other men seemed to concur. Marjorie left for Paris in January 1939, leaving their son at a school in Switzerland.

Mark remained preoccupied with his falling weight, his depression and his headaches. His last show opened in May 1939 to bad reviews. He visited Marjorie in Paris in May, and she told him that she did not plan to return. They decided to sell the house.

Although Mark had been solitary for much of his working life in the 1920s, Mark now felt lonely. Many of his friends were gone. Lady Ottoline had died in 1938, his friends had drifted away, and only Kot continued to visit. Mark gave up trying to paint. The events in Europe boded ill for Jews. Early in June, Mark attempted suicide with medication and gas, but changed his mind and survived.

He tried to visit his brothers on June 23, but they were busy. They agreed to meet the following week. Mark arranged to meet a women friend that evening instead. On the morning of the 23rd, an agent came to value the house. After the agent left, Mark went into his studio, locked the door, and lay on a mattress next to the gas ring and gas stove. He was found dead in the evening.

Discussion

Mark's life was characterized by constant depressions and migraine headaches. Although he did have tuberculosis, the postmortem showed that it had healed. Thus, his problems seemed to have been mainly psychological.

Although he had many close friends throughout his life, he failed to find an intimate partner with whom to share life. He fell in love with Dora Carrington and would have married her, but she was not in love with him. And even had she loved Mark, her own psychological stability was in doubt. As a consequence, Mark ended up at the age of forty alone in the world. As his friends began to die or move away, Mark was left alone. His parents were dead, and his brothers not sufficient to provide a reason for living.

Mark had always struggled with his painting. The periods of neglect more than outweighed the periods of acclaim, and he was never really a successful artist during his lifetime. The artistic developments on the continent overwhelmed the art world and left almost all of the British painters out of the mainstream. Mark himself was continually plagued by doubts about his merit as a painter and, since painting was so central to Mark's identity and existence, failure or even mediocrity was difficult to accept.

At the time of his suicide, then, Mark was facing the dissolution of his marriage, doubts about his artistic ability, and a further succession of severe depressions and his other symptoms. And he no longer had his beloved mother to provide him a reason for living. He appears to have lacked the resources for coping with the situation he was facing, and death seemed to have provided a resolution.

Vachel Lindsay[5]

Vachel Lindsay was a poet known mainly for reciting his poems. He embarked on numerous tours of the USA, so many that he grew tired of reciting the same poems time and time again. Eventually, at the age of fifty-two, he killed himself by drinking a bottle of lysol.

His Early Life

Vachel's family came originally from Scotland, but Vachel's father was born in Kentucky. He earned enough money to pay for his own medical training, became a doctor, and established his practice in Illinois. In 1871, when he was twenty-seven, he returned to Kentucky to marry his long-time sweet-heart, but found her dying from tuberculosis. He married her nonetheless, but she died within months after the wedding. He returned to his practice in Illinois. In 1875, he went with his sister and a friend of hers on a trip to Europe. He fell in love with the friend (Kate Frazee) and married her in 1876. Kate was from Scottish and English stock, and her father had worked as a farmer in Indiana.

When Kate was twelve, she was overcome by the sun while picking blackberries. Her sight was injured, and she seems to have developed some unspecified psychological problems after her recovery. She went to college, graduated with perfect grades, and taught mathematics in college for a while.

The Lindsays moved to Springfield and had six children. Olive, Vachel, Isabel, Esther, Eudora and Joy. Vachel (christened Nicholas Vachel) was born on November 10, 1879. When Olive was twelve and Vachel ten, Isabel, Esther and Eudora died within three weeks of one another of scarlet fever. The loss of the children was felt strongly, and the family visited their graves every Saturday.

Vachel came down with milk poisoning when he was four months old and remained ill for over a year. His mother kept him with her all the time, and this set up an especially close bond between them. His father was an intimidating figure. He warned Vachel strongly about the evils of venereal disease, drink and tobacco, and these prohibitions remained powerful edicts in Vachel's mind.

Vachel grew up to be an affectionate and excitable boy. His mother was the dominating parent in the household, but her husband was secure enough not to mind her authority. For punishment, Vachel's mother

---

[5] This section is based on Ruggles (1959).

would whip him with a light pony whip, but on one occasion, after he and some friends had accidentally burnt down some farm buildings, his father flogged him severely.

Vachel's mother was seen by townspeople as eccentric and a social climber. She took lessons in elocution, played the piano and painted. After the death of her three young children, she threw herself into social and religious activities. She taught Bible classes, became president of the Woman's Missionary Society of her church, and much more.

The Lindsays' house was plain and simple, but filled with books. Vachel joined the Disciples Church when he was ten and wrote his first poem on a religious subject soon thereafter. His grandfather had spoken of poets as clever but crazy and told Vachel that writing poems was something you did for fun as a hobby. His mother wanted Vachel to paint, and so she tried to convince him that his talent lay in art. Throughout high school he painted and wrote poems. Vachel always had a girl-friend, though she was needed for artistic inspiration rather than erotic purposes. Indeed Vachel remained a virgin until his marriage at the age of forty-five.

However, it was soon clear that both parents wanted him to become a doctor eventually. His father once gave him a skeleton in pieces and told him to learn how to assemble it. Vachel never succeeded, but he did enjoy sketching the bones.

He won prizes for his essays, enabling him to skip seventh grade. At the end of high school his mother sided with his father over his choice of career. He went off to college to become a doctor, though he wanted to become an artist. Vachel's mother had held Olive back a year so that she and Vachel could start Hiram College together in 1897. Vachel was not quite eighteen, Olive just under twenty.

The Young Adult

During his first year of college, Vachel wrote for the college paper and the college annual and continued writing poetry. His mother, though, continued to stress that writing poetry was at best a recreation. He tried out for basketball, baseball and football and failed at all of them. He failed also at the oratorical contests at the college. In these, his anxiety interfered with his performance, as it did in class and in social situations. However, he became a leader in college pranks.

He did not like his course of study. In his junior year, he skipped almost all his classes. He read literature and pursued his artistic inclinations. He decided that he wanted to become a professional illustrator or designer, with writing as a hobby until he could make his writing pay enough to live on. He dropped out of college after his junior year with the hope of enrolling at the Art Institute in Chicago.

Vachel stayed with his parents for a few months and arrived in Chicago in January 1901 when he was twenty-one. His father had fallen chronically ill with diabetes and had a ulcerous eye. The family remained in financial difficulties for the rest of his life but continued to support Vachel. Vachel attended classes at the Art Institute and earned some money by teaching classes at the local Disciples Church. When funds ran low, he would make do with a ten-cent lunch for the whole day. He wrote poetry every night but all of it was rejected by the editors to whom he submitted it.

Vachel's teachers were not very impressed by his skill, and he made few friends. He searched for a job with a newspaper and then with advertising agencies, but he was turned down by all of them. Finally, he took a job in a toy store as a stock boy but, after two months of working from eight-thirty in the morning till midnight, he quit. In June 1903, Vachel decided to go to New York to study art. His parents reluctantly agreed to support him in this.

While at Hiram College, he had grown attached to another student, Ruth Wheeler, and on the way to New York Vachel stopped in Akron and became unofficially engaged to her. In New York, he enrolled in the New York School of Art and continued to write poetry. He spent a lot of time at the Metropolitan Museum of Art and attended the Disciples Church regularly. Finally, he had two poems accepted in the Critic.

Back home in 1904 for Olive's wedding, he began to have visions which he saw as projections of his visual imagination. One night, he saw the prophets of the Old Testament pass though his bedroom. He spent six months in Springfield in a fever of imagination, constructing a cosmic system which he called his "universe", drawing an elaborate map of this imaginary realm and then writing about it in poems. He put all his work together in a book, Where Is Aladdin's Lamp, which was never published, but he made one copy to show others. Back in New York, in 1905, he abandoned his art education to concentrate on writing.

It is difficult to know exactly what Vachel experienced during this period. Nowhere does his biographer mention the possibility of schizophrenia, but this period seems to mark the beginning of more serious psychiatric problems than Vachel had ever shown before.

Vachel's Adult Life

Vachel decided to have two of his poems printed at his own expense. He wandered around New York, reciting the poems to shop owners and people he encountered, trying to sell them for two cents, and then trying to give them away. He found few takers.

He broke off his engagement with Ruth. He said that if he had an income he would marry her, an argument he used later when he was in love with Sara Teasdale, but he did nothing to earn any money. Now, and for many years more, he was content to live off the small amounts his parents could give him and the little he earned.

By October 1905, he finally had to take a job, and he began work in a factory. However, soon thereafter the YMCA paid him to teach classes in art, and he quit the factory. In 1906 he decided to go on a walking trip, and in the next six years he went on three such trips. He would have some of his poems printed and perhaps organize one copy of a book with poems and drawings. Then he would set off on a cross-country walk, staying with farmers and whomever would put him up, entertaining them in the evenings with recitation of his poems and those of others or showing them his book.

On his first trip in March 1906, he began in Florida with a friend, Edward Broderick. But Broderick soon deserted him, and Vachel continued his hike by himself, arriving at his Aunt's house in Kentucky two months later.

In the Fall, Vachel was again in New York, teaching for the YMCA and at settlement houses. In the Spring of 1908, he set out for his second hike, from New York to Springfield. After this hike, he decided to stay in Springfield.

In Springfield, he began to develop the idea that Springfield could become a model city for America and, indeed, the world. He lectured for free at the YMCA and began to formulate plans for a utopian city where culture and godliness would take priority over industry and commerce. He wanted to clean up town politics, build town pride, develop the talents of the gifted children, and build a city that would be an architectural wonder. He got involved in social issues too, speaking in favor of prohibition and socialist ideals. His delivery was crude, but he was acquiring the skills that would make him a fine public orator in later years. He continued to have romantic attachments, but one of his partners commented that Vachel never got beyond stroking her hand.

During this period, he continued to write, and beginning in 1909 he had several small leaflets printed at his own expense. These contained his utopian ideas, stories and poems. Vachel mailed copies of these to everyone he knew of in the literary field. Some of those who received them wrote suggesting other potential recipients.

Eventually, Vachel was noticed. One of his leaflets was reviewed in the Chicago Evening Post in 1909. One of his poems appeared in the Illinois State Register and was reprinted in papers throughout the Midwest. His work was accepted in Collier's and reviewed in Current Literature, and Vachel was invited to Chicago to meet the Cliff Dwellers, an association of regional artists and writers.

But for every acceptance, Vachel received many rejections, and he earned very little. His father's practice was not bringing much money, and so his parents rented out rooms in their house. Vachel even took a job as a laborer briefly.

In May 1912, Vachel set out for California on his third hike, but this time he had to take temporary jobs as a farm laborer to get by. The heat and the work were hard on him, and he often collapsed. But did make it to the family's camp on Mount Clinton in Colorado. After staying with them, he continued his walk west, but soon gave it up and wired his father to send him money for the train to Los Angeles.

In California, beginning to head back for home by train, Vachel was depressed, homesick, feeling persecuted by his family for being a poet, and ashamed that he had failed in his life. These feelings were always worse when he lost his inspiration and could not write. He came home to Springfield in October 1912, on the eve of his thirty-third birthday.

Fame

In 1912, Harriet Monroe, editor of Poetry in Chicago, noticed Vachel's poems. Soon, Poetry was publishing Vachel's work, and his writing was appearing in all the major publications. In 1913, Poetry awarded Vachel a prize of $100. Macmillan began to publish his books.

Vachel's poems were emotionally stirring with a strong rhythm, and Vachel's recitations of them were well-received. At a Cliff Dwellers' dinner in March 1914 in honor of William Butler Yeats, Vachel recited his poem The Congo to a rousing reception. Thus began Vachel's series of recitations of his works that lasted until his death. Vachel recited to all kinds of groups, at most of the major universities, and even to President Wilson and his cabinet. Eventually, Vachel experimented with accompanying the readings of his poems with dance and pantomime.

Vachel loved the response of an enthusiastic audience. Yet he also grew tired of being called upon to recite the same poems time and time again and of the lonely travel from town to town to the engagements his agent had arranged for him. Still, these tours provided his major source of income, and his poor financial position, especially after his marriage and the birth of his children, compelled him to go on more tours.

He continued to write poems and to editorialize on political and social issues (he was a pacifist for the first part of the First World War), and he produced some innovative critical works. For example, his book in 1915, The Art Of The Moving Picture, suggested for first time that films might be considered an art form.

Romantic affairs continued to cause problems for Vachel. He had fallen in love with Octavia Roberts in Illinois, but she rejected his proposals of marriage several times. He then began to correspond with Sara Teasdale, eventually met her and fell in love with her. But she too rejected him. Next, in 1917, at the age of thirty-seven, Vachel fell in love with Isadora Bennett who was 17. When she rejected him to marry a soldier, Vachel was very upset.

Decline

After 1920, Vachel's fortunes began to decline. His work which had hitherto been well received seemed to be poorer in quality. A strange book which he had thought would be his masterpiece, The Golden Book Of Springfield, was ignored by critics. New poets were coming along, like T. S. Eliot, and they received critical attention. Increasingly, Vachel found it hard to write. The long and exhausting recitation tours that he undertook, partly to satisfy his desire for approval and partly for the money, left him little time to write. But also, his creativity seemed to be drying up. In later years he would sit for hours trying to create a new poem or write an article for a magazine that might earn him money, but he produced little.

His father died in 1918 and his mother in 1922. Vachel had lived his life dependent upon them. He had depended upon their financial support, and he had returned to live with them after his few years in New York. Their deaths were a great loss to him. (He had felt very ambivalent toward them. He both loved and felt hostility for his mother, yet wanted her recognition for his accomplishments.)

For most of his life Vachel was lonely. He had few friends back in Springfield. Men thought him strange, and women seemed to tolerate him only a little. However, he continually fell in love with them in his eccentric way, only to be rejected by them. His views too often left him without friends. His pacificism during the First World War eventually became an unpopular position. His travels left him alone in hotel rooms in strange cities.

As he grew older, more and more symptoms appeared. After a trip to England with his mother in 1920, he lost his vitality, cried easily and acted silly and excited over nothing. Sometimes his handwriting was sprawling and uncontrolled. Later, his letters became rambling, with misspelled words and aborted sentences. He had spells of depression, vertigo and what his biographer calls 'dazed dullness'. He was often angry. Politically, he turned against the immigrants whose entry into America he had once welcomed. Now he wanted them sent back. He behaved badly toward those hosting him, often shouting abuse at them for which he would have to apologize afterwards. He began to talk about his 'enemies' in America who were glad that he seemed to have written himself out.

In January 1923, after a recital near Gulf Park Junior College for Girls, he broke his tour to rest and recover, staying with the President of the College whom Vachel had known at Hiram College. He began to teach at the college and stayed for eighteen months.

He fell in love with an eighteen year-old student there who, as usual, rejected him. He found the students boring and uninterested in intellectual topics. He began to talk of enemies among the faculty who disapproved of him and spied on him. His brother-in-law came down to see what was wrong with Vachel and found him hallucinating and distraught. Vachel talked continually about his persecutors and argued that America owed him a living. In June, 1924, his brother-in-law took him to the Mayo Clinic where Vachel was diagnosed as having epilepsy. Vachel eventually admitted that, as a child, he had awoken at night on the floor to find his tongue bitten half through. But having the affliction labelled as epilepsy was a shock to Vachel, and he never accepted the label or forgave his brother-in-law for taking him to the Mayo Clinic. Vachel was prescribed luminal sodium by a neurologist.

Vachel's biographer was content with this diagnosis. However, even if we assume that Vachel may have truly had epilepsy, few epileptics develop paranoid delusions or hallucinate. Today, such symptoms would be viewed as signs of schizophrenia, and once we see these signs as schizophrenic in nature, much of Vachel's strange life makes sense. His inability to finish college or to find and hold a job, his bizarre relationships with women, his obsession with religious-political causes and his unrealistic goals for his home town of Springfield suggest a pre-psychotic personality disorder.

But Vachel was also depressed. After the deaths of his parents, he suffered from insomnia, felt very lonely and wrote to friends that he could find no reason for continuing to live. Friends described him as weary, worn, inexpressibly sad and antagonistic toward his audiences.

Vachel decided to move to Spokane in Washington, where he moved into a hotel, subsidized by an admirer who wanted to improve the cultural life of Spokane but who never let on to Vachel that he was paying part of his hotel bill. In Spokane, his biographer describes him thus:

> His swinging, ungainly gait was more marked than
> ever. He carried a cane, wore his cowboy hat and
> often dancing pumps.....and he lifted his face as
> though to taste the universe, then lowered it
> to note with shrewd eye some sign of the times.
> (Ruggles, 1959, p. 333)

In February 1925, Vachel met Elizabeth Conner, a twenty-three year old school teacher in Spokane. He still wrote to his girl friend from Gulf Park Junior College and even sent her an engagement ring. When she firmly said no, Vachel proposed to Elizabeth.

Vachel's eccentricity is illustrated by this decision. Elizabeth was teaching on a Tuesday morning in May, when the minister arrived to tell her that Vachel proposed to get married that very day. Elizabeth, who had known nothing of this, acquiesced, and they were married at nine in the evening after Elizabeth returned from an AAUW meeting!

Vachel's biographer reports that the marriage was happy and gives no hint of any sexual difficulties. Elizabeth did not know of Vachel's seizures when she married him. He had a seizure in August while they on a hiking tour, and Elizabeth, who was now pregnant, felt very anxious about what was in store for her.

Vachel decided that he would like to move back to his parents' house in Springfield. His paranoia had spread to include people in Spokane. During a speech to the Spokane AAUW, he began to talk of the businessmen in Spokane who were trying to drive him out of town and crucify him. Vachel managed to move his family back to Springfield and into his family home in April, 1929.

Money was scarce, and Elizabeth could not meet expenses. Vachel continued his recitation tours to bring in money. Despite his tours, from which he sent back less and less money to Elizabeth as time progressed, money remained scarce, and the family ran up bills with local merchants. A daughter was born in May, 1926, and a son in September, 1927.

His new books received bad reviews, and Vachel was upset by this. Since Vachel had already developed paranoid tendencies, these attacks fed into his delusions of persecution. He complained about his critics and the publishers who were now rejecting his work. He sat at home in Springfield trying to write, but writing little. He began to drink, he who had spoken in favor of prohibition, and he smoked heavily. He was jealous of any man who visited Elizabeth, and accused her of infidelities. He continued to tour, but spent more money during the tours and sent less home to Elizabeth. (In 1929, his income was $11,628 of which $1,022 was from royalties and rents from the Lindsay estate. The rest was from recital fees. $2,387 went to his agent, but after deductions for expenses, only $3,293 remained.)

Although Vachel still received honors (a prize from Poetry and an honorary doctorate from Hiram College), these were based on his past accomplishments, not on present endeavors.

In February, 1931, he was diagnosed as having a mild case of diabetes mellitus, and the additional stress caused Elizabeth to tell Vachel how she felt about him and their life and to declare that she would not sleep with him any more. (Vachel's biographer says she did not keep her vow.) On his tours now, his self-control was gone. He refused to recite the poems his audiences wanted, and he screamed at his hosts. He wrote rude letters to his sisters, and Elizabeth felt that some of his letters indicated madness.

Vachel began to threaten Elizabeth with physical violence, even that he would kill her. Eventually, he did assault her mildly. He accused his father-in-law of trying to murder him. Vachel's brother-in-law considered institutionalizing Vachel and consulted with psychiatrists, but Vachel refused to visit any psychiatrist or neurologist.

In November, 1931, Vachel's debts totalled $4,000, and he was on the road again. He was fifty-two. In November, he was giving a recital in Washington, DC, when the amplifiers broke down and many in the audience left. Vachel, however, was not aware of the technical difficulties, and the exodus of the audience troubled him greatly. When he arrived home on November 29th, his speech was thickened, he seemed dazed and his hands were shaking. After his first night at home, he asked

Elizabeth who she had met in the house during the night. (There had been no visitors.)

On December 4th, Vachel was depressed and crying. Later that day, he attacked Elizabeth, accusing her of taking away his pride. He talked about his life, recalling every hurt and working himself into a tearful fury. After they went to bed, Vachel got up and swallowed a bottle of Lysol. Elizabeth sent for a doctor, but Vachel died soon after the doctor's arrival, at one in the morning.

Discussion

There is no evidence of psychiatric disturbance in Vachel's family, except for the psychological problems his mother experienced after her sunstroke. His childhood seems uneventful except for the death of his sisters when he was ten.

Yet during his college days the first signs of his adult life style began to be evident, a life style that can be characterized by an inability to develop any kind of career, to support himself, or to develop mature interpersonal relationships. It is interesting that his parents supported his aimless life-style despite their own financial difficulties.

As he got older, Vachel began to show more of the symptoms of severe mental disturbance, in particular hallucinations and delusions of persecution. Aside from any possible epilepsy, Vachel seems to have developed schizophrenic symptoms, complicated by depression.

Interestingly, like Ernest Hemingway, Vachel distorted the circumstances of his life. As a child he had wished that he had Indian blood in him, but as an adult he insisted that he did. He denied that he accepted money from his father when in fact he had. After his father's death, he claimed he supported himself and bought his mother everything she wanted, whereas the truth was that he borrowed heavily from her. He implied that he had been fired or forced into resigning from Gulf Park Junior College, whereas he had refused to return.

Toward the end of his life, his psychological state became much worse. His creative life seemed over, critical rejection of his work grew, and the stress of the recitation tours increased. He was unable to relate rationally to anyone, including his wife. He was severely depressed. If he had not killed himself, Vachel would probably have had to be institutionalized.

Since he left no suicide note, we can only speculate about his personal motives for his suicide. But his biographer says that Vachel told Elizabeth after swallowing the lysol: "I got them before they could get me - they can just try to explain this, if they can!" (Ruggles, 1959, p. 432). It appears that Vachel killed himself under the influence of the delusions that people were trying to kill him, and he thwarted them by killing himself first.

Cesare Pavese[6]

Cesare Pavese was born in Italy in 1908, and he killed himself at the age of 42 in 1950. During that time, he became a leading intellectual, editor, translator, poet and novelist.

His Early Life

Cesare was born on a farm in Santo Stefano Belbo in the Piedmont province of North Western Italy (which borders on Switzerland and France). He often returned to his home town in later years, and Pinolo Saglione, a carpenter there, remained a friend and confidante.

Cesare was born on September 9, 1908, and it was by chance he was born on the farm since his parents lived in Turin and visited the Pavese family farm only in the summers. Cesare's father, Eugenio, worked in Turin at the Court of Justice. Cesare's mother, Consolina, was the daughter of wealthy merchants. Cesare had a sister, Maria, six years his elder. (Consolina had lost three children before Maria and Cesare, the first dying of diphtheria at the age of six.)

Cesare's childhood was spent in Turin during the Winter and Spring and at the farm in Summer and Autumn. Cesare developed an affinity and a liking for the country and, though he lived most of his adult life in cities, was really a country boy. He longed for the summers when he could escape Turin for the farm.

When he was six, the family was about to return to Turin when Maria caught an infectious illness that forced the family to stay on the farm. Cesare attended first grade in the country school, but the next year began attending a private school in Turin.

More importantly, when Cesare was six, his father died from a brain tumor that he had suffered from since before Cesare's birth. Cesare felt a great sense of loss, but he was ashamed of his tears and choked them back.

Cesare's mother, long tried by tragedy, was not warm or tender but rather showed her love by working hard for the family. She was thrifty and kept a tight rein on her children. She forbad talk over meals and forced the children to eat everything she served. Cesare began to withdraw from her, and their relationship became increasingly cold.

Cesare had lost his father and was not close to his mother. He began a lifestyle of being alone, even when among others, and of feeling

---

[6] This section is based on Lajolo (1983).

sad. He was more attracted by misfortunes than by celebrations. His father was a dreamer and an avid reader of books, and soon Cesare began to follow his father's interest. He hated his school books but loved literature. Yet, Cesare was not lonely. He had playmates at the farm and a small circle of friends at school.

Though he loved literature, his report cards usually described him as intelligent but lazy. After elementary school, he attended a Jesuit junior high school for a year but could not fit in with the spoiled and snobbish children of the wealthy. After three years, he switched to a public junior high school. His eyesight was poor, and he needed to wear glasses. He was tall, but slender and frail, walking with a slouch. He usually had a bad cough in the Winter, and soon he developed asthma.

Cesare's life was also inextricably interwoven with the rise of fascism in Italy. In 1922, fascist groups burned the trade union headquarters and two socialist clubs in Turin. Communists and trade unionists were arrested and assassinated. Fascism exalted arrogance, boldness, action and a political philosophy that Cesare could not accept. He detached himself from fascism and withdrew more into himself and his studies.

As a consequence, he began to pay attention to his teachers, to study, to write and to enjoy his school. He studied Greek by himself, and visited the public library frequently with his friend, Mario Sturani, reading all he could.

High School and College

Cesare entered the lyceum (high school) in 1923 at the age of fifteen. He soon was a member of group of friendly students, and he came under the influence of a teacher of literature and Latin, Augusto Monti, a teacher whose students became his disciples and life-long friends, who incidentally disliked the fascists and whose students tended also to become anti-fascist.

Cesare passed the hard entrance exam to college, and his college years were filled much as the lyceum years with literature, discussions, and writing. The group of students from the lyceum stayed together and still met with their old teacher, Monti. But the group grew larger. In this environment, Cesare seemed happier than ever before. He began to appreciate films and to translate American authors into Italian. His thesis was on Walt Whitman, and initially it was rejected because his professor viewed it as a political attack on fascism. Cesare managed to change professors and graduate.

The fascists rose to power, led Italy into the Second World War on Germany's side, and were overthrown. The Germans then attacked the Italians. After the war, there was much political fighting between the various groups, especially the communists. Cesare's friends and colleagues were involved. They joined the resistance, became political, and fought for what they believed was right. Where was Cesare in all of this?

Sitting in on the discussions to be sure, but rarely saying anything. He did not join the resistance. He lived out the war in the countryside, away from the fighting. He finally joined the communist party, but was never active. He did <u>nothing</u>.

Lajolo, his biographer, characterizes Cesare's novels well. They are about vagabonds, drunks and idle people. The characters spend their lives in taverns, drinking and talking. They have no occupation, are without love, addicted to drinking and smoking, satisfied to wander the streets aimlessly all night, and in the end they sink into melancholy. This is Cesare.

It is perhaps not true to say the Cesare did nothing. He wrote, poems, novels and essays that intellectually supported left-wing ideas. Even his translations of American literature can be seen as challenges to the fascist regime by introducing Italians to the American ideals of freedom of thought and speech. So he worked tirelessly in these endeavors. And he was exiled for ten months by the fascists and was under surveillance for much of the time. But even Cesare knew that he was avoiding the real fight. At the end of the war, when he learned that friends had died fighting for the ideals he supposedly supported, his feelings of being a failure were amplified.

His Career

A few months after receiving his degree, Cesare's mother died. Although they had not been close, she had represented his roots and given him a sense of security. To replace her, he moved in with his sister and her family, where he lived for the rest of his life.

In order to earn some money, he worked at translating, mainly American novels, but a few English ones also. He chose books with subtle (rather than obvious) political significance. He was not allowed to teach in the public schools because he refused to join the fascist party. He could teach only in temporary and substitute positions, in private schools and as a private tutor.

In 1933, he began to work for a new publishing company, the Einaudi Publishing House, started by a former student of Augusto Monti. Cesare helped to decide which foreign works to translate into Italian and worked at getting the appropriate permissions. The publishing house was under suspicion by the authorities, and on May 13, 1935, Cesare's home was raided. He had at home a letter from a left-wing prisoner which he refused to explain. He was tried and sentenced to three years exile, though he was released after ten months.

His exile was spent in Brancaleone Calabro, in Southern Italy (at the toe). He was dependent on money sent to him by his sister, and he spent the time there lonely and bored. His asthma was bad, and he hated the sea and the winds. Eventually, his letters became angry and bitter, full of complaints.

He was released after only ten months, but was crushed upon his return to Turin to find out that a woman he loved had just married someone else. He fell into a severe depression. His first book of poems had not been received with any enthusiasm, and he no longer saw writing as worthwhile. What got him out of his mood was taking on a student for lessons in Greek and Latin literature. They met at 7.30 every morning for an hour, and eventually Cesare regained his enthusiasm for literature. He began work again at Einaudi, eventually helping to set up their office in Rome.

From 1928 to 1932 Cesare had been occupied primarily with translations, from 1932 to 1937 with writing poetry, but from 1937 until his death he wrote short stories and novels. He continued his writing during the war.

He was drafted into the army in March, 1943, having been previously excused because he was the son of a widow. However, when they discovered his asthma, he was sent to a hospital and for six months convalescence. The fall of the fascist regime saved him from service. When he returned to Turin, most of his friends had left to join the partisans in the Resistance War against the Germans. Cesare went to stay with his sister in the country, where he once more immersed himself in literature. His diaries from this period contain no mention of political events or the war.

After the war, he returned to Turin and began work again at Einaudi's. He found that many of his friends had died in the fighting. He finally joined the Communist Party, perhaps as a way of redeeming himself.

By 1947, he seemed serene and happy. He was working, dictating his novels to a colleague at Einaudi, Maria Livia Serini. But after each novel was completed, Cesare would become physically weak, asthmatic, and bitter and depressed again. He soon lost Maria Livia who was transferred to Rome.

By 1948, Cesare was very nervous and anxious. He could not tolerate solitude in the city. So he hurried off to Santo Stefano Belbo, his old home, to visit with Pinolo Scaglione. He returned to Turin, went to Rome, returned to Turin. His sister became accustomed to him disappearing every week end. In his novel Among Women Only published in 1949, he described the way in which he would later kill himself. (Suicide had been, however, a constant theme in his writing.) He began to worry about headaches and whether he had a brain tumor like his father. He smoked medicinal cigars to ease his asthma. He talked of his agitation, palpitation, sense of decay, and insomnia.

In June, 1950, he was awarded the Stega Prize for his new novel, The Beautiful Summer. But by late August he was dead.

Women

After the poor relationship he developed with his mother, it is not surprising that Cesare had problems with women in his life, problems which became the major sources for his depression.

Let us look at his first school-time crush, Olga. He tried to speak to her but felt too shy and inhibited. So he watched her from afar. He felt inferior to her, a simple country boy with big hands and poor vision, while his friends socialized with ease with their girl friends. One day he was walking by the river and saw a boat with the name Olga written on it. He turned white and fainted.

A second revealing incident happened while he was at the lyceum. One day, Cesare found the courage to ask a singer at a cabaret out. They set a date for six in the evening, to meet at the front of the club. Cesare arrived punctually at six. He waited and waited. At eleven, the rain began, but still he waited. At midnight he returned home, sad, humiliated and freezing. He learned the next day that she had left via the back door with another admirer. The depression and fever led to pleurisy which put him in bed for three months. Later he would write much about his philosophy of life in his letters, his diary, and his novels. Writing to a friend, he once asked, "Don't you agree that no joy surpasses the joy of suffering?" We can see this clearly in his stubborn wait outside that club for six hours.

Lajolo is rather coy about Cesare's love life. Perhaps he visited prostitutes. It certainly seems as if Cesare was impotent, most likely ejaculating prematurely and so rarely satisfying his lovers. It may also be that his penis was overly small.

There were three major loves in his life, all of whom rejected him. The first is named by Lajolo 'the woman with the hoarse voice'! She was studying mathematics at the university and is described by Lajolo as firm, cool, strong-willed and good at sports. While he was with her, Cesare was more natural, human, tender, and confidant than ever before. But she betrayed him, leaving him bitter and never again trusting women. Lajolo does not tell us whether Cesare and his friend were lovers.

Lajolo tells us, without giving examples, that Cesare rejected maternal or submissive women, as well as those that loved him. Rather he fell in love with and pursued those who did not love him, strong women with minds of their own, perverse and unfaithful. Cesare wrote, "The only women worth the trouble of marrying are those a man cannot trust enough to marry."

When Cesare was in exile, the woman with the hoarse voice rarely wrote to him. On the day he returned from exile, he was met at the train station by his friend, Sturani. He asked after her. Sturani told him that she had been married the previous day. Cesare fainted. Though she married another, it is important to note that before Cesare's exile, her lover was in prison and they communicated by letters sent via Cesare. (It was one of these letters that he was tried and exiled for.) She had never been faithful to him, and Cesare had been willing to accept this! From the train station he went to his room in his sister's house and stayed there for days. He refused to eat, he did not read, and he thought of suicide. But he lived on.

In 1940, Cesare met Fernanda Pivano and was in love with her for five years. They met almost daily, and he would read her poems and novels. He asked her to marry him one day, but she did not reply. In all of those five years, Cesare never kissed Fernanda! Eventually she married someone else.

In Rome in 1945, Cesare met a woman who aroused his passion. Lajolo is again coy, and we learn nothing save that Cesare made "an attempt to prove his virility. Once again he was dissatisfied and returned to his silence and to self-destructive thoughts. Back in Turin he wrote, "Again alone...you make your house in an office, in a cinema, keeping your jaws clenched."

The final woman in his life was an American actress visiting Italy, Constance Dowling. As soon as he met her, he began to fear her desertion. Eventually he saw her as a flirt (and she did go to bed with a fellow actor). In July 1950 he was with her in Milan and appeared 'blissful'. Constance went back to America, and Cesare awaited a telephone call from her saying she would marry him. It never came.

Depression and Suicide

Cesare began to be depressed early in his life. His failures with women exacerbated these feelings and precipitated the most severe depressions. Depression would also develop after he had completed a novel, suggesting that his writing kept his depression at bay.

Throughout his life he talked about feeling worthless. This idea focussed on his failures with women. No matter how much he wrote or how enthusiastically it was received, he would compare himself with those who were married and had children and consider himself a failure. And his impotence! He wrote, "...a man who ejaculates prematurely should never have been born....it is a defect that makes suicide worthwhile."

He described his life as a fight with depression that he had to fight "every day, every hour, against inertia, dejection, and fear." In 1927, he wrote to his friend Mario Sturani saying that he was incompetent, timid, lazy, weak and half-mad. Should he kill himself or not? But he did not have the courage to kill himself. He was a child, a cretin, a 'poseur'. More probably, he said, he would masturbate himself to death. Don't cheer me up, he wrote. Let me enjoy my depression in peace.

While he was at the lyceum, a friend, Baraldi, and his girl friend went to the mountains where they shot themselves. Baraldi died; his girl friend lived. Within a few days, Cesare decided to imitate Baraldi. He took a gun to the same town, Bardonecchia, but could not kill himself. He fired the shots into a tree instead. Cesare does not seem to have attempted suicide at all before his death.

In August 1950, his sister, staying in the country, was worried about her brother, so she returned to Turin. She found him frighteningly thin, his eyes hollow and red. For two days he burned letters, documents and photographs. He left his light on all night. But he became calm, patient and even kind. On the morning of Saturday August 26th, he asked Maria to pack him a suitcase as if he was going away for one of his weekend trips. He went to the Hotel Roma in town. On Sunday evening, a hotel employee was worried because the guest had not been seen all day. He forced the door open and found Cesare lying on the bed dead, dressed except for his shoes. On the night stand were sixteen empty packets of sleeping pills. His last words in his diary read, "All this is sickening. Not words. An act. I shall write no more." On the cover of one of his books by his bed in the hotel room, he had written, "I forgive everyone and ask forgiveness of everyone. O.K.? Not too much gossip, please."

An Absurd Vice

Lajolo called his biography of Cesare An Absurd Vice, which is how Cesare described his obsession with suicide. Cesare's life is easily summed up. An intellectual, enthusiastically concerned with issues in literature, but aware that such issues take second place to the common needs of all people - finding love and a place in the world.

Cesare's disposition and childhood experiences (the death of his father and his unaffectionate mother) prevented him from becoming mature. He never left home, moving from mother to sister, living all forty-two years with them. He never developed the social skills necessary for relating to women. He knew Fernanda for five years, proposed marriage, but never kissed her. She would have been foolish to marry such a man unless she was as immature as he was.

Cesare had friends, but listen to what he says. "As soon as I am aware that a friend is getting too close, I abandon him. I abandon women, those whom you call maternal, as soon I deceive myself into thinking they love me." Cesare cannot stand closeness. It scares him. At another time he writes, "(Cesare) wants to be alone - and he is alone - yet, at the same time, he yearns to be in the center of a group which is conscious of his solitude." He is alone, even when with friends.

Indeed, his intellectual concerns about literature, which formed the topics for his conversations and his many essays, are ideal ways for having with contact with others while remaining distant. This is no different from the friends we have who talk of nothing but their work or the politics of their work place.

His fears over his impotence were probably unfounded. With the little sexual contact he had, no wonder he ejaculated prematurely. If he had made love to Fernanda (or someone else) every day instead of reading poems to her, his sexual behavior may have developed normally. But the initial failures led to shame and to anxiety that he would always fail. And the shame and anxiety probably made him fail in the future. It became a self-fulfilling prophecy, a prophecy made more likely by falling in love with women who rejected him. It is hard to make love to a woman who hurts you and towards whom you feel anger.

Cesare suffered from depression all of his life. He frequently thought of suicide and eventually killed himself.

Lajolo gives us no hints of a history of depression in Cesare's family. Though Cesare lost his father when he was six, his father had been ill all along, and so the death may not have been unexpected. His mother was cold, but she clearly cared for her family. Cesare's childhood was not ideal, but far from being as traumatic as some childhoods. It is surprising that such moderately disturbed settings lead to such misery. Or perhaps Lajolo has not told us all?

Mark Rothko[7]

Mark Rothko was born as Marcus Rothkovich on September 25, 1903, in the city of Dvinsk in what would later be called Latvia. His father, Jacob was a wealthy pharmacist. Marcus had a sister Sonya fourteen years older, a brother Moise eleven years older and a brother Albert eight years older. Perhaps he was unplanned?

After Mark's birth, his father became more religious, and, whereas the older children had gone to the public schools, Mark was sent to the Jewish school. Dvinsk was spared the pogroms against the Jews in Russia, but the fear of persecution led the family to plan emigrating to America. Jacob arrived at Ellis Island in 1910 and went to Oregon to join his brother there. His two older sons escaped to America through the underground (to avoid serving in the Czar's army), and in 1913 Jacob sent the money for his wife and Mark to come.

They settled in Portland, Oregon, as the Rothkowitz's, but Jacob died after seven months. Sonya had a degree in dentistry but could find work only as a cashier. The older sons worked for their uncle until they learnt English well enough to pass the examinations in pharmacy. Mark went to the public schools and worked hard selling newspapers before and after school.

Mark later recalled that he never had time for play, and his brother Albert remembered him as a tense and sensitive boy who was perpetually hungry. Mark grew to be the giant in the family, five foot

---

[7] This section is based on Seldes (1978).

eleven tall. He finished high school by the time he was seventeen and developed an early reputation as a defender of labor and radical causes.

In 1921, Mark set off for Yale University on a full scholarship. Mark studied hard and worked to meet expenses, first as a waiter and then in a laundry. However, after six months, Yale took away his scholarship. (Mark's biographer points out that Yale University discriminated against Jews.) Mark was told that he must borrow the money from Yale if he wanted to attend, and Yale dunned Mark for many years for the money he owed.

After two years, Mark decided that he had had enough of Yale, and he quit. He moved to New York City and got various jobs to get by. He happened to find himself at a drawing class one day when he went to meet a friend there, and he was intrigued. In January 1924, he joined the Art Students League, and he sampled classes there for the next two years.

During the late twenties, Mark illustrated maps for books but ended up suing the publisher for royalties he had been promised. He lost in court. In 1929, Mark taught part-time at the Center Academy in Brooklyn, and he continued to teach on and off for the next thirty years to supplement his income from painting, much as he disliked teaching.

At the Catskills for a holiday he met Edith Sacher, also from Brooklyn. They fell in love and married. It was a mismatch. Mark was a melancholic romantic Russian with the desire to be a painter. Edith was pragmatic and built up a business as a jewelry designer.

The Depression brought rewards, for Roosevelt's programs included the Federal Art Project. Mark had had exhibitions of his work in Portland and New York in 1933, and in 1935 he was hired by the Project. One result of the Project was to bring artists together in collective groups. Mark was part of a group of dissidents who attacked the establishment. They got attention but sold few paintings.

Mark became a citizen in 1938 and in the 1940s changed his name to Marcus Rothko. (He later changed it to Mark Rothko.)

Mark had begun painting representational paintings of city scenes and then switched to surrealistic seascapes in watercolor. This early work was successful but sold poorly and was barely noticed by the major art critics. During the Second World War, he and Edith divorced, and in 1944 he met Mary Alice Beistle (known as Mell), an illustrator of children's books, Protestant and from Cleveland. They married in 1945.

The Rise To Fame

After the war, the artist's community in New York City remained tightly knit, with Mark belonging to the uptown group. Their life was consumed by art, producing it and discussing it. In 1946, Mark had his surrealistic seascapes on show in San Francisco and Santa Barbara. He also taught at the California School of Fine Arts for two summers.

In 1947, he began to explore new directions for his paintings and produced misty forms of color suspended in space. Eventually, his style of paintings, along with the works of other contemporaries, became known as the New York School of Abstract Expressionism. They opened a school of art and published periodicals. Mark sold his pictures to the Whitney Museum and to the San Francisco and Brooklyn museums. However, his total income from painting and teaching in 1949 was $3935, leaving him $1387 after paying for materials.

In 1950, Mark and Mell went on their first trip abroad (to England, France, and Italy), and Mell got pregnant. Kathy (Kate) was born at the end of the year. At this time, the marriage was happy. Mark's moodiness and cynicism appealed to Mell. To support the family, Mark gave up part-time teaching and joined the faculty full-time at Brooklyn College.

Mark's fame continued to grow. Still angry at the Whitney Museum for their lack of support of contemporary artists in the past, he refused to have his works exhibited there (though he had sold them some paintings), but he was included in a show at the Museum of Modern Art. However, he refused to let his works be shown abroad where he would have no control over how they were hung.

In the 1950s, dissension grew among the artists, and the group broke up, often with bitter feelings between the rising stars jealous of one another's success. In 1954, Mark had more shows and signed up with Sidney Janis as his dealer, yet his biographer notes that he had a take-home pay of only $2433. Mark was thrown into reliance on sales of his paintings when Brooklyn College denied him tenure. (Mark accepted visiting lectureships at the University of Colorado and Tulane for the following year.)

In the late 1950s, art collecting took off. Millionaires discovered art as an investment and tax shelter. Dealers proliferated, and prices soared. Works by Mark (as well as Willem de Kooning and Jackson Pollock) were mentioned by <u>Fortune</u> as good investments. (This led to jealously and broken friendships with painters whose names were omitted from the article.)

But at this time too, just when poverty was ending for Mark, his psychological state began to deteriorate. He had always been an insomniac and moody. But now his melancholic moods turned into depressions, and his moods ranged from one extreme to another. His friends described him as a volcano. Money became a worry to him now that he had some after years of poverty. On one occasion, the theft of his bank statements led to a bout of depression.

His drinking increased, and he developed hypochondria combined with a distrust of doctors. In 1956, he developed a fever and painful swollen joints. After three months in bed, he allowed a doctor to see him (but not take a blood sample). He had gout. When he finally permitted treatment, his doctor also discovered hypertension. But Mark declined to have regular medical checkups.

As his fame as a painter grew, Mark became increasingly concerned about what was written about him. He disliked being identified with the New York School. He disliked the comments made about his work by critics. He began to worry intensely about how his work should best be exhibited, both during his life and after his death.

However, his years of poverty were over. Mark and Mell bought a little cottage in Provincetown and were eventually able to move into better apartments and better studios. Bernard Reis became his financial advisor and worries focussed on taxes and how to avoid them. Mark was very frustrated over the structure of the art profession. Universities, museums and the art dealers all frustrated and angered him. Although some of his anger seemed excessive, abuses were indeed widespread. Favoritism was common, art dealers wrote contracts that exploited the artists, and financial advisers mismanaged their clients. (For example, Franz Kline lived with difficulty on $5000 a year until his death in 1962, although his dealer/adviser had $200,000 in account for him.)

Despite the abuses of the system, Mark's income increased dramatically during the 1960s. He bought a house for $75,000 on East Fifty-Ninth Street. He found a good studio (in the East Sixties). He sold paintings both through dealers (eventually working with Frank Lloyd and Marlborough Galleries) and independently. In 1961, he was invited to the Kennedy inaugural. His paintings were fetching $20,000, and he had a retrospective at the Museum of Modern Art: fifty seven paintings.

In 1962, Mark became acutely depressed. His brother Albert had cancer, and the art world was turning to "Pop" art as the new fad. In late 1962, at the age of fifty-nine (Mell was forty-one), he had a son, Christopher.

In 1964, John and Dominique de Menil commissioned Mark to paint murals for a new chapel in Houston. This project occupied him for the next few years. When he finished in 1966, he had painted fourteen murals and eight experimental studies. The project dominated his life and drained him emotionally and physically. Visitors to his studio described him as pompous, self-centered, and hostile. He banished friends who failed to praise him sufficiently. One visitor recalls being criticized by Mark for conversing with him rather than immediately going to view the new paintings.

Mark continued to be successful financially. He limited sales of his paintings to keep their prices high, and for those he sold personally he demanded cash. In 1968, his murals for the Houston Chapel were ready, and the Tate Gallery in London had purchased an earlier set of murals he had painted. But then one day he felt a pain in his back, and his legs went numb. He had suffered an aneurysm of the aorta, brought on by arteriosclerosis and hypertension. He stayed in the hospital for three weeks, and, though he recovered physically, he remained psychologically upset by this illness.

His depression intensified, and his health became an obsession. His egotism turned into self-pity, guilt and doubt. The mistrust he had for the art world became paranoid. His alcohol abuse worsened. His anger began to focus more on Mell, and the marriage deteriorated. (He loved flirting with other women, and his biographer reports that he had three serious affairs during his marriage. Unfortunately, one of his lovers told Mell about her affair with Mark. Thus, the marriage had seen problems all along.) Mell was tired of tending to this self-centered, drunken genius, and she too turned to alcohol. Mark began to think of separation.

He also began to plan for the Mark Rothko Foundation, the focus of which was primarily to preserve his work and to arrange for its display and prominence after his death. Mark wanted to ensure his fame and prominence in the future, and the foundation was the center of his plan for immortality in the art world. The foundation would keep the works together and arrange exhibits in proper groupings in suitable lighting. However, this work on the Foundation also depressed him since it brought home the imminence of his death.

As his drinking (and cigarette smoking) increased, his depression worsened. Bernard Reis took him to see Dr. Nathan Kline who specialized in tranquilizers and antidepressants. Kline gave him Valium and a new antidepressant in addition to the pills Mark was taking for hypertension, gout and insomnia.

By the end of 1968, Mark had a rebellious teenage daughter (Kate was seventeen), a rambunctious five-year old and an unhappy, alcoholic wife. Mark moved out on New Year's Day, 1969, to his studio. He still supported the family financially, returned for laundry and occasional meals, and checked on his family all the time. He began seeing a widow, Rita Reinhardt, who entertained hopes of marrying him, but it appears that he was impotent in the later years of his life. It appeared also that he feared being finished (impotent) as an artist. Although now a millionaire, he lived frugally, like a pauper.

He next worked on a series of paintings of blacks on grays that many visitors saw as signs of impending doom. He became more dependent on his friends, needing their approval of his paintings, fearing abandonment. He needed people for lunch and to talk to at odd hours. Friends were forced to disconnect their telephones at night to avoid being awakened. At meals with the family, there would be fights over Rita and the food Mell served him. His daughter found him usually depressed and uncommunicative.

Still successes continued. In June, 1969, there was a Rothko room at an exhibition at the Museum of Modern Art. The price for his paintings reached over $50,000. In October, 1969, the Metropolitan Museum had a show of modern artists including ten of Mark's paintings, but the show angered Mark and exacerbated his self-doubt and fears for his stature in the art world.

During the summer of 1969, his mood worsened. During a visit to a doctor (Alan Mead) he was totally disoriented, disturbed and dazed. Mead cut his dosage of Valium and Mellaril, sent a report of this to Kline, and persuaded Mark to see a psychotherapist. But Mark would not enter therapy. His drunkenness worsened, even to the point of losing control of his bodily functions.

By November, Mark was desperate. He called his regular physician (Dr. Albert Grokest). Kline had given him new pills. Grokest was upset by this treatment that was independent of his own and told Mark not to take Kline's medication. Kline requested a meeting with Grokest, but Grokest refused to meet with him.

On January 27, 1970, Mark visited Mead because Grokest had gone to Mexico. He was taking large amounts of Valium. He could not work and felt pressured by his family and girl friend. He was impotent. He could sleep only with the use of chloral hydrate. He had a hernia, gout, and emphysema from chain-smoking. He was worried about his hypertension, but his blood pressure was normal. He was also getting medication from Kline. By February, his worsening eyesight added an extra stress. He seemed to be painting again, though he was demanding friends visit him. They noticed that his memory was deteriorating.

He had agreed to let the Marlborough Gallery enter his storehouse on Wednesday February 25th to select paintings to purchase. He had never allowed people into his storehouse. Mark had always made the selections himself. On Thursday February 19th he dined and fought with his family. Over the weekend, he seemed withdrawn and was seen sitting alone in Central Park.

On Tuesday he kept his appointment with Dr. Mead. His condition seemed a little better, but he was still agitated and depressed. He had an appointment with Kline on Friday. On Tuesday night he dined with Rita. She judged him to be full of rage and frustration over the selecting of his paintings the next day. Rita reassured him that he could refuse to let the gallery representatives see his storehouse.

At 9am on Wednesday, Mark's assistant (Oliver Steindecker) let himself into the studio. In the kitchen, he saw Mark stretched out on the floor. He had slashed his arms in the crooks of the elbows. It was suspected that he had taken barbiturates too.

Discussion

Mark's biographer suggests many motives for his suicide. He had deep self-hatred and rage against the world, his father had abandoned him to go to America when he was seven, and his son was now approaching seven (as was the child of close friend). Perhaps Mark could not accept the news about his health? Perhaps he was trying to get attention? He was torn between Rita and his family. His memory and eyesight were failing him. He was scared about his position in the art world.

However, what is noteworthy is his chronic depression. He had been melancholic all of his life, and his depression became severe toward the end. Apparently, the antidepressants were not effective in ameliorating it. His alcoholism made this problem much worse.

Second, Mark's insecurity about his prestige as an artist seems central to his state. Despite his fame and wealth from sales of his paintings and exhibitions all over the world, he seemed to fear that after his death his work would be ignored and forgotten. He seemed determined to prevent this, partly by building up his prestige before he died and by setting up a foundation to preserve his reputation after his death.

His deteriorating health, especially given his hypochondria, must have played a part in his suicidal depression. The fact that his psychological state worsened so much after his aneurysm supports this hypothesis. Mark must have expected to die soon.

His interpersonal life was in shambles - a lover with whom he was impotent, a family with whom he fought, friends who avoided him, and former friends whom he had cut off or who had cut him off.

In many ways, he resembles the aging and suicidal Ernest Hemingway, save that Hemingway was still married at the time of his suicide. Both were psychotically depressed, in failing health, and facing the end of their creative life. Both chose to escape rather than continue on to an imminent, painful and miserable dying.

References

Haffenden, J. The life of John Berryman. Boston: Routledge & Kegan Paul, 1982.
Lajolo, D. An absurd vice. New York: New Directions, 1983.
Ruggles, E. The west-going heart. New York: Norton, 1959.
Seldes, L. The legacy of Mark Rothko. New York: Holt, Rinehart, & Winston, 1978.
Unterecker, J. Voyager. New York: Farrar, Strauss & Giroux, 1969.
Woodeson, J. Mark Gertler. London: Sidgwick & Jackson, 1972.

Chapter 8

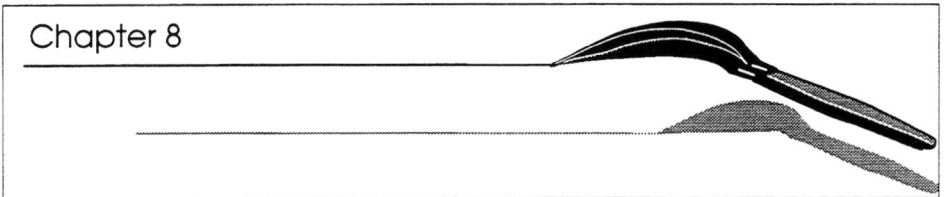

COMPARING THE SUICIDAL WOMEN AND MEN

In this final chapter we will compare the lives of six female artists and writers who committed suicide with the lives of six male artists and writers who committed suicide. As before, let us first begin with some simple demographic information.

Name	Birth	Death	Age	Birth order
Diane Arbus	3-14-1923	7-26-1971	48	2nd of 3
Dora Carrington	3-29-1893	3-11-1932	38	4th of 5*
Sylvia Plath	10-27-1932	2-11-1963	30	1st of 2
Anne Sexton	11-9-1928	10-4-1973	44	3rd of 3
Sara Teasdale	8-8-1884	1-30-1933	48	4th of 4
Virginia Woolf	1-25-1882	3-28-1941	59	3rd of 4
John Berryman	10-25-1924	1-7-1972	57	1st of 2
Hart Crane	7-21-1899	4-27-1932	33	only
Mark Gertler	12-9-1892	6-23-1939	46	5th of 5
Vachel Lindsay	11-10-1879	12-3-1931	52	2nd of 6*
Cesare Pavese	9-9-1908	8-27-1950	41	2nd of 2*
Mark Rothko	9-25-1903	2-25-1970	66	4th of 4

The women and men did not appear to differ in their age at the time of the suicide, their birth order or whether they completed suicide at a time close to their birthday (indicated by an *). With regard to birth order, three of the ten suicides were first-borns or only children while five were last-borns.

Name	Marital status	Children	Parental death
Diane Arbus	divorced	2	none
Dora Carrington	tonsingle	0	none
Sylvia Plath	separated	2	father/8/natural
Anne Sexton	divorced	2	none
Sara Teasdale	divorced	0	none
Virginia Woolf	married(1st)	0	mother/13/natural
John Berryman	married(3rd)	2	father/11/suicide
Hart Crane	single	0	(grandfather/13/natural)
Mark Gertler	separated	1	none
Vachel Lindsay	married(1st)	2	(sisters/10/natural)
Cesare Pavese	single	0	father/6/natural
Mark Rothko	separated	2	father/10/natural

As we noted when comparing the suicidal and nonsuicidal women, separation and divorce characterizes these suicides (rather than widowhood). For the men, in addition to those already separated (Gertler and Rothko), two of the remaining marriages were in severe trouble (Berryman and Lindsay). In fact, of the ten suicides, only Virginia Woolf was securely married.

As we noted in Chapter 5, early loss is often found in the lives of suicides. This is especially true for the men. Three of them had lost parents (the father in each case), and two others had lost close relatives with whom they were living (a grandfather in one case and sisters in another). As Bron, et al. (1991) have recently noted, loss of the father seems to be especially important in the histories of suicides, and loss of the father was more common in these samples of suicides than loss of the mother.

Name	Method Used	Prior Attempts/Age
Diane Arbus	Barbiturates	None
Dora Carrington	Gun	Car Exhaust/38
Sylvia Plath	Domestic Gas	Poison/20
Anne Sexton	Car Exhaust	Several Overdoses
Sara Teasdale	Poison	None
Virginia Woolf	Drowning	Jumping 22/Poison/31
John Berryman	Jumped	In front of train/16
Hart Crane	Drown at Sea	Wrists/Poison/16/32
Mark Gertler	Gas	Wrists/Medication/46/49
Vachel Lindsay	Poison	None
Cesare Pavese	Poison	None
Mark Rothko	Wrists	None

As with the women, a fair proportion of the male suicides had made prior nonfatal attempts and half had shown evidence of alcohol and drug abuse. The psychiatric state of the men seems even worse than that of the women. Four of the men had depressive disorders and two more had depressed mood. One was schizophrenic (Lindsay). Interestingly, two new symptoms appear in the men, two of whom may have had epilepsy and three of whom showed signs of paranoia (delusions of persecution). These symptoms were absent in the women.

Name	Psychiatric Disorder
Diane Arbus	Depressive Disorder
Dora Carrington	None
Sylvia Plath	Depressive Disorder
Anne Sexton	Depressive Disorder/ Substance Abuse/ Hysteric Neurosis
Sara Teasdale	Depressed Mood
Virginia Woolf	Depressive Disorder
John Berryman	Alcohol/Drug Abuse/ Epilepsy/Depressed Mood
Hart Crane	Alcohol Abuse / Paranoia/Depressive Disorder/Homosexual
Mark Gertler	Depressive Disorder
Vachel Lindsay	Schizophrenia/Epilepsy/ Depressed Mood Paranoia
Cesare Pavese	Depressive Disorder
Mark Rothko	Depressive Disorder/ Paranoia / Alcohol Abuse

The Role That Creativity Played

We saw in Chapter 5 the women were affected by the reception their work received. To reiterate, of the six suicides, Dora Carrington appears to have lost confidence in her ability as a painter, Sylvia Plath had just published her first novel to luke-warm reviews, Sara Teasdale was experiencing severe writer's block, and Virginia Woolf was acutely anxious in the time leading up to publication of her novels and depressed afterwards. [1] This seems to have been true for the men also.

John Berryman's life was disintegrating because of his uncontrollable alcohol abuse. His confidence in his ability to write had gone, and he no longer had the discipline to finish any creative work. He had a profound lack of self-confidence, preferring to teach undergraduates rather than critical graduate students. Although he had received awards for his writing, his aspirations increased. Once it was sufficient for his work to be published. Then he needed praise, and next to be seen as the greatest living poet. Toward the end of his life, he needed extravagant praise for each draft of a potential poem and could no longer tolerate minor criticism. There were other contributing causes to his suicide, including his continuing inability to stop his alcohol abuse and his disintegrating marriage (primarily a result of his alcoholism).

Hart Crane had struggled hard to get his poetry accepted. His work, when published, often received critical reviews. Furthermore, his lack of education and his abusive personal style made it difficult for him to broaden his scope and write essays or reviews to any great extent. He achieved some recognition and success, eventually obtaining a Guggenheim fellowship. At this point, his personal life and alcohol abuse resulted in an almost complete inability to write. It was likely that he would never produce a major work again. In addition, his alcohol abuse and his inability to form a lasting intimate relationship with anyone, homosexual or heterosexual, provided important motivations for his suicide.

Mark Gertler seems to have been affected by his creative work. He had doubts about his worth as an artist, especially in comparison to the dynamic trends in art taking place in Paris and the rest of Europe, led by Picasso and Matisse, and had been depressed and suicidal. His interpersonal crises and physical health added to this career stress and made suicide even more likely.

Vachel Lindsay had never been a very good writer. Most people agreed that he was best as a reciter and performer of his own work. His later writing was criticized as quite poor, and Vachel continued to be in demand only as a reciter. His suicide seems determined by his deteriorating relationship with his wife brought about by his psychotic behavior, ending with violent assaults, and the stress resulting from the

---

[1] Diane Arbus and Anne Sexton seemed least affected by their creative careers

continual demand to keep touring and reciting in order to support his family.

Cesare Pavese was depressed after each novel had been completed, but he had developed many avenues of work in the field of literature, including publishing and reviews. His suicide, though, seems to be a result of his inability to form lasting relationships with women. He had ended up as a grown man living with his sister, suffering rejection from the women he was infatuated with and enduring loneliness and depression.

Mark Rothko seemed to be less concerned with doubts about his stature as an artist than with how his art would be viewed after his death. The establishment of a foundation to own, preserve and exhibit his art became a dominant concern to him. His suicide, however seems to have been more motivated by his disintegrating marriage and his physical and psychiatric health.

The creative work of four of the male suicides, therefore, seems to have a played a role in their suicide (Berryman, Crane, Gertler and Rothko). This influence was weaker in Lindsay's suicide and barely present in Pavese's suicide.

Conclusions

It is clear that depression, both of psychiatric proportions and of moderate intensity, played a role in almost all of the suicides committed by the writers and artists discussed in this book.

It is clear also that concern over their worth as writers and artists played an important role in the suicides of many of these people, regardless of their gender. In this, therefore, we are supporting beta bias, so named by Hare-Mustin and Marecek (1988), of concluding that women and men are similar. (Alpha bias is assuming that women and men are different.) Despite the prejudice and sexism that women artists and writers faced in their lives, there seems to be no clear evidence from their biographies that the sexist nature of society contributed to their suicides. Of course, this lack of evidence does not prove that sexism did not play a role, for the biographies may have been biased against documenting such sexism. Nonetheless, the factors of early loss, interpersonal difficulties, psychiatric disorder and concerns over their value as writers and artists appear to have been the major etiological factors in the suicides of both the creative women and the creative men.

References

Bron, B., Strack, M., & Rudolph, G. Childhood experiences of loss and suicide attempts. <u>Journal of Affective Disorders</u>, 1991, 23, 165-172.

Hare-Mustin, R. T., & Marecek, J. The meaning of difference. <u>American Psychologist</u>, 1988, 43, 455-464.

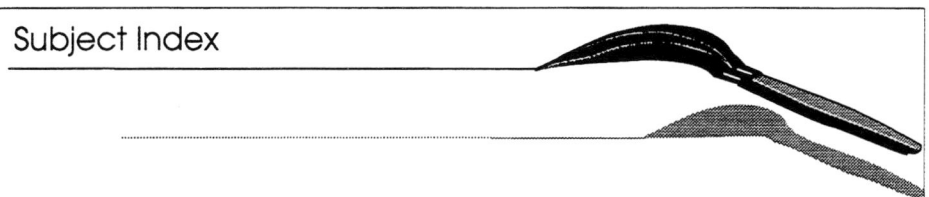

Subject Index

A Critical Fable, 72
A Dome of Many-Colored Glass, 69
A Few Figs FromThistles, 76
A Star Is Born, 25
Abels, Cyrilly, 38
Adams, Franklin Pierce, 23
Adler, Felix, 30
Affective Disorders, 95
Ainslee's Magazine, 76
Alchoholism, 94
Algonquin group, 23
Algonquin Hotel, 23
Allyn, John, 102
Ames, Beatrice, 24
Ames, Lois, 48
Amitola, 81
Among Women Only, 139
An Absurd Vice, 142
Angus, John, 103-104
Antioch Review, 46
Arbus, Allan, 30
Arbus, Diane, 29-35, 151-155
Art Students League, 81

Balzac, 61
Beistle, Mary Alice, 144
Bell, Clive, 19
Benchley, Robert, 23-24
Bennett, Isadora, 131
Berlin Academy of Art, 11, 14
Berlin School of Art for Women, 13
Berlinski, May, 122
Berryman, John, 101-111, 151-155
Between the Acts, 21
Bibesco, Marthe, 65
Big Blonde, 24

Birth Order, 91-92, 151
Bishop, John, 76
Bloomsbury circle, 20
Boissevain, Eugen, 77-78
Boyd, Nancy, 76
Boys Foundation School in Whitechapel, 123
Broderick, Edward, 130
Brunner-Orne, Dr. Martha, 44-45
Bruno's Weekly, 112
Bry, Doris, 86, 87
Bynner, Witter, 71, 75, 76

Cambridge University, 39-40
Campbell, Alan, 24
Campbell, Bhain, 110
Cannan, Gilbert, 124
Carrington, Dora, 7-10, 15-16, 122, 124, 151-155
Chabot, Maria, 86
Cheri, 65
Children, 92-93
Claudine and Annie, 62
Claudine At School, 62
Claudine in Paris, 62
Claudine Married, 62
Cliff Dwellers, 131
Colette, 61-67, 151-155
Colette Willy, 63
Colette, Jules, 61-62
Colette, Sidonie Gabrielle, 61
Collins, Seward, 24
Conklin, Margaret, 51, 56, 58
Conner, Elizabeth, 133
Cowley, Peggy, 115
Crane, Hart, 111-120
Creativity, 95-96, 154-155
Critic, 129

SUBJECT INDEX

Crosby, Harry, 115
Cummington School of the Arts in Northampton, 30
Currie, John, 123

de Comminges, Isabelle, 64
de Jouvenal, Colette, 64
de Jouvenel, Henry, 64
de Menil, Dominique, 146
de Morny, Mathilde, 63
de Reme, Lily, 64
Debussy, Claude, 62
Dell, Floyd, 76
Dialogues de Betes, 63
Dicke, Ann, 31
Dickinson, Violet, 19
Dictionary of National Biography, 17
Die Sezession (The Secession), 12
Disciples Church, 128
Donahue, Kate, 106-107, 109
Dow, Caroline, 75
Dowling, Constance, 141
Dream Drops, 68
Duse, Eleanor, 72
Dwyer, Ada, 70

Edinburgh Review, 17
Einaudi Publishing House, 138
Eliot, Alex, 30
Elizabeth Arden Beauty Salons, 86
Eminent Victorians, 8
Engel, Carl, 70
Enough Rope, 24
Esquire, 25
Ethical Culture School, 30
Evans, Ross, 25

Fashion Photography, 31-33
Fatal Interview, 78
Faure, Gabriel, 62
Federal Art Project, 144
Ficke. Arthur, 71, 75, 76, 78
Fieldston School, 30
Filsinger, Ernst, 54, 56
Fir-Flower Tablets, 72
Forum, 75
France, Anatole, 62

Free Congregation, 11
Friday Club, 121

Garland School in Boston, 44
Garrett, John, 24
Gauthier-Villars, Henri, 62
GEDOK, 14
Gertler, Mark, 8, 120-127, 151-155
Gide, Andre, 65
Glamour, 31
Goncourt Academy, 66
Goudeket, Maurice, 65
Gray, Mary, 43
Greenfield, Patti, 34
Gretor, Georg, 13

Hamilton, Juan (John), 87-88
Harvey, Anne, 43
Hatfield, Stafford, 53
Headlam, Walter, 19
Hemingway, Ernest, 34, 97, 135, 149
Heriot, Auguste, 64
Hippopoetess, 71
Hodgkinson, Marjorie, 125
Hogarth Press, 28
Holley Hotel, 77
Holmes, John, 45
Horney, Karen, 34
Hudson Review, 46
Hughes, Ted, 39-40
Hunt, Leigh, 68
Imagination and Fancy, 68
Imagists, 69
Israel, Marvin, 33

Jewish Educational Aid Society, 121

Kahn, Otto, 117
Kayo, 44-48
Keats, 68, 73
Kimmel, Jess, 34
Kollwitz, Karl, 11
Kollwitz, Käthe, 10-16, 151-155
Kongisburg Academy of Art, 11
Koteliansky (Kot), S. S., 123
Kumin, Maxine, 45, 48

SUBJECT INDEX

Lady Ottoline Morrell, 123
Lawrence, D. H., 70, 123
Lawrence, Katherine, 67
Le Matin, 64
Legends, 72
Levine, Ann, 106
Levinson prize, 46
Lightfoot, Maxwell, 121
Lindsay, Vachel, 54, 57, 127-136, 151-155
Little Boy Blue, 75
Lloyd, Frank, 146
Lotz, Myron, 37-38
Love, Desire and the Chimera, 63
Lowell, Amy, 62-74, 151-155
Lowell, Augustus, 67
Lowell, Robert, 31, 46, 97
Luhan, Mabel, 85

MacArthur, Charles, 23
Mademoiselle, 38
Makler, Lina, 12
Manic Trends, 97-98
Maniez, Marguerite, 63
Mansfield, Katherine, 123
Marital Status, 92-93
Mark Rothko Foundation, 147
Marlborough Gallery, 148
Marquise de Belbeuf, 63
Marsh, Edward, 123
Mauer, Rudolf, 11
Mauriac, Francois, 65
McClain, John, 24
Mercy Street, 47
Millay, Cora, 74
Millay, Edna St. Vincent, 72, 74-80, 151-155
Minne, 63
Minneapolis Institute of Art, 34
Mitsou, 65
Model, Lisette, 32
Monroe, Marilyn, 34
Mulligan, Eileen, 106
Museum of Modern Art, 33, 146

Neide, Emile, 11
Nevinson, C. R. W., 8, 121
New English Art Club, 122

New Secession art group, 14
New York School of Abstract Expressionism, 145
Newsom, Jerrie, 87
Night and Day, 21
No, Siree!, 23
Norman, Dorothy, 84-85

O'Hara, John, 53
O'Keeffe, Georgia, 80-89, 151-155
O. Henry Prize, 24
Orne, Martin, 43

Parental Death, 92-93, 152
Parker, Dorothy, 21-26, 26-28, 151-155
Parker, Edwin, 22
Parrish, Williamina, 51
Parson's School of Design, 33
Pavese, Cesare, 136-143, 151-155
Peasant War of 1525, 13
Plath, Otto, 35
Plath, Sylvia, 35-43, 151-155
Poet Lore, 52
Poetry, 46, 69, 117, 131, 134
Poetry Society of America, 52
Pollitzer, Anita, 87
Potters, 51
Pound, Ezra, 69
Prince Ernst Heinrich of Saxony, 15
Prisoners, 13
Proust, Marcel, 62
Prouty, Olive, 37
Provincetown Players, 76
Prussian Academy of Arts, 14
Psychiatric disorder, 94-95, 153

Radio City Music Hall, 85
Rahv, Philip, 49
Red Cross, 78
Reedy, William, 52
Reis, Bernard, 146
Rejection, 95
Retreat from Love, 63
Rittenhouse, Jessie, 51, 53, 75
Robert Levitt Award, 34
Roberts, Octavia, 131

SUBJECT INDEX

Robineau-Duclos, Jules, 61
Ross, Harold, 23
Rossetti, Christina, 57
Rothko, Mark, 143-149, 151-155
Rothschild, Mrs. Henry, 21
Rothstein, William, 121

Sacco, 24, 78
Sacher, Edith, 144
Saglione, Pinolo, 136
Saxton Foundation Grant, 40
Schizophrenia, 133
Schmidt, Kathe, 10-16
Schober, Aurelia, 35
Serini, Maria Livia, 139
Sevenels, 70
Sexton, Alfred, 44
Sexton, Anne, 43-50, 151-155
Shearman, Monty, 124
Shelley Memorial Prize, 46
Shelton Hotel, 84
Sherwood, Robert, 23
Simplizissimus, 13
Slade School of Art, 121
Smart Set, 75
Smith College, 37-39
Snodgrass, W.D., 46, 97
Social Democratic Workers Party (SPD), 11
Some Imagist Poets, 71
Spanish Civil War, 25
St. Nicholas, 75
Stage Relief Fund, 78
Stanley, Marion, 51, 53
Steepletop, 77
Stega Prize, 139
Steindecker, Oliver, 148
Steinem, Gloria, 87
Stephen, J. K., 18
Steuben Glass, 86
Stieglitz, Arthur, 81-86
Strachey, Lytton, 8-10, 20, 71, 122
Strand, Beck 85
Sword Blades and Poppy Seeds, 70

Taylor, Deems, 77

Teasdale, Sara, 50-59, 131, 151-155
Thackeray, Harriet, 17
The Art of the Moving Picture, 131
The Beautiful Summer, 139
The Bell Jar, 37-38, 41
The Bookman, 24
The Bridge, 117
The Congo, 131
The Golden Book of Springfield, 131
The Harp-Weaver and Other Poems, 77
The Innocent Libertine, 63
The Monthly Story-Teller, 68
The New Yorker, 24
The Pagan, 113
The Potter's Wheel, 51-52
The Voyage Out, 20
Toomer, Jean, 85

Untermeyer, Louis, 75

Van Doren, Mark, 104
Vanity Fair, 22, 23, 76
Vanzetti, 24, 78
Venice Biennale, 34
Vogue, 22
Volney Hotel, 25-26

Wague, Georges, 63
Weaver's revolt, 13
Westbeth, 34
Wheeler, John, 54
Wheeler, Ruth, 129
Wheelock, John, 54
Where Is Aladdin's Lamp, 129
White Buildings, 117
Wilkinson, Marguerite, 51, 57
Willard, Buddy, 37
Wilson, Edmond, 76
Woolf, Virginia, 17-21, 26-28, 151-155
Woollcott, Alexander, 23
Writers War Board, 78
Writing, 96-98
Writing Creativity, 95
Yaddoo, 40